# THE GIRL ON THE LEFT

A HEART-CENTRED ANTHOLOGY OF EMPOWERING STORIES

## MEGAN DIRKS

ALONG WITH 21 AMAZING WOMEN

# TABLE OF CONTENTS

# WELCOME TO THE GIRL ON THE LEFT
## A NOTE FROM PROJECT CREATOR, MEGAN DIRKS

Hey you. Yes, you. I'm Megan Dirks, the creator behind *The Girl on the Left*, and if you're holding this book, I need you to know: You belong here.

This project has been living in my heart for almost five years, and it's so much more than just a book to me. It's a challenge and a love letter to growth, self-acceptance, and radical love for the messy, imperfect versions of ourselves that we often try to forget.

The girl you want to crop out of old photos.

The one who made mistakes, struggled, and doubted herself.

The one you swore you'd never be again.

For the longest time, I tried to leave my own girl on the left in the past. I thought she was something to be embarrassed about. It took me almost a decade to look back and realize she wasn't the problem. She was the whole reason I made it here and paved the way to a life I now unapologetically love.

We've all seen the shiny before-and-after stories. We live in a world where the "after" is polished and perfect, and the "before" just needs fixing. But what about the often unpictured work in the middle? The late-night pep talks, the ugly cries, the tiny choices that changed everything?

This book flips that script.

It's a celebration of the girl who kept showing up when it was easier to quit.

The one who dragged herself to the gym when she wanted to stay in bed.

The one who learned to set boundaries, say no, and walk away when it mattered.

The one who chose growth over comfort, vices, and old patterns, even when it sucked.

Self-development pushes us to always level up, but we don't talk enough about honoring the person who got us here. That girl in your before photo? She wasn't broken. She was messy, resilient, and exactly who you needed to become who you are today. She wasn't perfect, but she was *real*.

This anthology is a celebration of the versions of ourselves we try to overlook. It's not just a collection of stories, it's a rapidly growing movement. We all have a girl on the left, and it's time to give her the love she deserves.

Inside, you'll meet 21 incredible women who've done just that. They've looked back at their past selves and said: "You were amazing, too." I'm deeply grateful to them for trusting me with their stories.

To the women who shared their stories: You're rockstars. This book wouldn't exist without you.

To you, the reader, know that every author on these pages came together to inspire self-love and growth. We handpicked themes to be diverse, relatable, and to remind you that you're not alone. No matter your age, background, or beliefs, this project is for *all women*.

As you read, think about your own girl on the left. Take a loving look at the version of you who may have been messy, unsure, or lost, but who kept going anyway.

Every step you've taken has led you here.

Every version of you has mattered.

You are enough, exactly as you are.

Thank you for being here and embracing your own story. Together, we're proving that every version of ourselves deserves love.

With love, impact, and all the big dreams,

# TRANSFORMATION

## A GOTL POEM BY NATHAN FRAUGHTON

Past shapes future
Who we once were
Who we've become

With battles hard fought
A journey once taken
Melds two into one

Dreams of a future
Need courage and heart
To take the leap

Into the unknown
Up mountains high
And valleys deep

To build a dream
From ashes comes life
Chance to discover

Trial by fire
Is what it takes
Journeying from one to another

When the fight is through
Look back with pride
At the self you've grown from

She carried you here
The girl on the left
Now your time has come

# MEGAN DIRKS

## GAMING, WELLNESS & ENTREPRENEURSHIP

I've always been someone who pursues goals with a mix of curiosity, rebellion, and sheer persistence. I'm bold, resourceful, and often take on challenges that others shy away from—not to seem cool or edgy, but because I've learned time and time again that following the crowd isn't always the best path.

I had a very loving childhood. My parents were separated, and while finances were sometimes tight, I was always surrounded by care and a strong sense of community from family, neighbors, and friends. My circumstances weren't exactly unique, but as I grew older, I started to notice that the environment around me was shaped by a mindset I didn't have the words for at the time—scarcity.

People were doing their best, but many were caught in cycles of struggle and coping in ways that left them feeling stuck. Childhood itself was wonderful, but adolescence was a wake-up call. It was during those years, as I became older, that I started to understand things like coping mechanisms, mental health, escapism, and mindset traps.

Art, music, and later gaming became my creative outlets—pathways that fueled my big, bold dreams for what could be. But gaming didn't remain just a hobby; it gradually became a crutch, a way to escape when life felt too overwhelming. Unfortunately, that was almost always. In those formative years, rather than building a solid foundation, I relied on gaming too much, turning what should have been a passion into a major vice.

It's wild how the things we love most can sometimes become the very thing that derails us. For me, video game addiction and an incredibly late PCOS diagnosis were the twin battles that shaped the person I am today.

The experiences I want to share here taught me lifelong self-assurance, sparked my creativity, and showed me the power of rewriting your own narrative—even when it feels impossible.

I saved for my first $500 secured credit card to gain independence for travel, booking hotels, and renting apartments. I also saved $200 to close the gap between my two front teeth, a small but persistent insecurity. When braces weren't an option, I researched composite bonding, pitched it to my dentist, and made it happen. These early steps built my self-assurance—I didn't wait for anyone to make things happen. I researched, hustled, funded, and followed through. Each win made me think, "Maybe my life really can be whatever I want it to be." I was driven to break free and do things differently. With limited resources, I had to be smart and strategic, but that only made me more determined.

* * *

Living with undiagnosed polycystic ovarian syndrome (PCOS) as a teenager felt like being trapped in a mystery—both the detective and the victim. PCOS, a hormonal condition, causes symptoms like fluctuating weight, infertility, and absent periods. At the time, I didn't know what it was, but its effects shaped how I saw myself and interacted with the world.

Physically, I didn't get periods. At first, people just called me a late bloomer. But as time went on, it became clear something wasn't right. My body wasn't maturing the way I expected, and the confusion and frustration of not knowing why weighed on me. Other signs began to emerge, like male-pattern facial hair growth. It wasn't just the unexpected hair—it grew fast. I could have a full beard in a week if I didn't keep on top of it. It wasn't just about appearance; it severely impacted my confidence and relationships.

Emotionally, it equally sucked. The weight gain, facial hair, and lack of answers made me feel like a failure on every level. Depression slowly crept in, and I withdrew from the world. By my late teens and early twenties, I was living in survival mode. While my peers were dating, starting to have sex, and building lives, I felt stuck on the sidelines. Even if someone found me attractive, I couldn't see it myself. Vulnerability, especially when it came to intimacy, felt impossible.

The fallout didn't stop at my personal life. My reclusiveness bled into other areas, like a full stop of progress in school, work, and finances. I escaped into video games for about two years, shutting out the world because facing it felt pointless.

* * *

At that time, video games consumed me, filling a void I didn't know how else to handle with little resources. I started playing World of Warcraft on a trial and eventually paid for a subscription. In my head, it seemed practical—my friends were spending hundreds of dollars on nights out downtown drinking, and I was spending $20 a month for endless entertainment.

I justified my spiral by pointing out that it was better than getting pregnant early or hanging out in sketchy areas and drinking with friends. In the game, I found a sense of accomplishment and community I lacked in real life. I had direction, goals, and a social circle that valued me for who I was, not for my appearance or my flaws.

I formed lasting friendships with people from around the world, some of whom I'm still close with to this day. We celebrated birthdays, shared our struggles, and spent hours talking. These friendships weren't based on superficial judgments; they were genuine connections that made me feel seen and appreciated. I was thriving in the virtual world—rich in the game's economy, valued by my team, and suddenly fulfilled. Meanwhile, real life felt like a constant reminder of my shortcomings.

Naturally, I spent more and more time in the space where I felt good and avoided the one where I didn't. Makes sense, right? Except, now I know to spot that as addiction at its finest: Avoidance. Overconsumption. Justification. Denial.

* * *

Eventually, I recognized the need for balance. I found a youth support program that offered a six-month work term at a bottle recycling depot. It wasn't glamorous, but it was a start. The program was designed for youth facing significant challenges—many of my peers had histories of crime or addiction. I didn't entirely fit the mold, but the staff saw my desperation and gave me a chance. That job was a lifeline, teaching me basic skills like customer service and cash handling while giving me a routine. I continued gaming to counter my anxieties and insecurities, but at least now I had some cash flow and forced balance.

From there, I moved into a series of temp jobs, each one slightly better than the last, but none truly fulfilling. My confidence was still shaky, and I was battling internal struggles that still stemmed from the PCOS. Frustrated by my body's refusal to change despite my strict diet and exercise, I spiraled into unhealthy eating habits. I restricted calories to the extreme and started purging in certain situations, rationalizing it as "strategic." I knew it wasn't sustainable, but I felt desperate for control. No matter how carefully I followed all the rules—eating "right," taking supplements, hitting the gym for hours each day—my body still refused to cooperate, leaving me feeling trapped and hopeless.

* * *

Then, I met someone—a guy I'd connected with online. He loved me as I was, which was something I hadn't expected. His support gave me the stability I needed to start piecing my life together. He encouraged me to pursue college and was willing to help me financially to make it happen. Even as I moved forward, I still struggled with my own self-worth. But for the first time, I felt like I had a partner who truly believed in me, even when I didn't believe in myself.

The wild part? I actually went for it—I took on the scary student loans and chased my passion for art. I combined my love for art and gaming and enrolled in a 3D Art & Animation program. The dream? To work at a game studio, designing cool characters or epic monsters and getting paid to be part of that creative world. But life had other plans. The very specific private college I chose had both of my instructors drop out within the first month of the program. We had 60 days to pull out and get a refund. I waited until day 59, no replacements had been found, and I made the tough decision to drop out while I was still eligible for a refund. Many of my peers were backed by their parents' money—I wasn't. I couldn't justify risking our future, especially so early in the relationship. So, I let it go. Added to my list of almosts.

Instead, my partner and I pivoted. We started learning to develop video games together, encouraging each other's growth. That was when I began to embrace the vulnerability I'd been so afraid of before—love, support, and the raw honesty that came with sharing our skills and dreams. It was a turning point, not just for my potential career, but for the kind of relationship I'd always wanted but never thought I deserved.

\* \* \*

Admittedly, we didn't live the healthiest lifestyle for a while. I was so frustrated by the lack of results despite my efforts that I eventually reached a breaking point—a "screw it, nothing I do matters anyway, so why not just order the damn pizza?" mindset.

Stepping on the scale and seeing 249 hit me hard. That number was my wake-up call. All these years, I'd built this narrative in my head that 250 was the point of no return—failure, despair, and no control over my body. I had toyed with the drastic idea of doing something stupid with suicidal thoughts if that metric became real. But thankfully, something inside of me snapped—not in a way that broke me, but in a way that made me furious.

I was done with this cycle of self-loathing and fear. I wanted to live. More than anything, I wanted to thrive. That moment wasn't about avoiding death—it was about demanding more from life. It was the catalyst that finally pushed me to fight harder for answers. I wasn't crazy. I wasn't lazy or weak. I was someone with a body that was working against me, and I needed the right team to help me figure it out.

Finding the right medical professionals was a whole journey in itself. I scoured resources, interviewed doctors, and learned to advocate for myself in ways I never had before. Eventually, I connected with someone who took the time to truly listen. We dug into my blood work, my history, and my symptoms. Piece by piece, we uncovered what had been wreaking havoc on my body all those years. It was a slow and frustrating process—trial and error with medications, diets, and therapies. But for the first time, I felt like I had a shot at gaining control.

Unfortunately, since we were about 10 years late in catching this as it developed, it was pretty much ruling my body, and the best chance to get a handle on it, even though I was so young, was bariatric surgery. That wasn't done locally, so my next crazy move was to go out of the country instead. My local area wasn't well-practiced in it, Canadian waitlists were absurd, and private practices were insanely expensive. The neighboring US had costs triple that, and I started digging deeper into the health tourism scene in Mexico.

There was so much stigma surrounding it. But at the end of the day, I knew it wasn't about appearances; it was about giving my body the reset it desperately needed. So, I took the plunge, traveling to Mexico to visit a surgeon who specialized in the vertical sleeve gastrectomy (VSG) procedure. It was terrifying, but it was also empowering. What it did was remove a portion of my stomach, forcibly readjust my hormone levels, and encourage me to be very mindful and nutrient-dense with the limited space I had.

The VSG wasn't a magic fix—it was a tool. But armed with that tool, suddenly, everything I had been doing started working. Clean eating and exercise weren't just futile efforts anymore; they were effective. My body was finally responding. Over the next year and a half, I lost over 120 pounds. I couldn't believe it. For the first time in years, I felt like I was just getting to know myself.

Of course, the journey didn't end there. No one tells you that massive weight loss comes with its own set of challenges. I ended up with a ridiculous amount of loose skin after what was considered a massive full-body weight loss. The loose skin wasn't just a cosmetic issue—it was a medical one. It was causing infections in my skin folds, irritation, and pain. It felt like trading one set of problems for another, but it had to be addressed.

That meant more surgeries, more recovery time, and more financial strain. Each procedure was a battle, and the timeline stretched across five years. I juggled freelancing, side hustles, and odd jobs, doing everything I could to fund my care while receiving occasional support. There were moments when it felt endless, but I refused to give up on myself. Said and done, I tackled over $100,000 in medical debt by the time I turned 28. I didn't even realize until the end of all of that how much I lived in a fight-or-flight response for over 10 years, just scrambling to make sure things stayed okay.

People thought I was a badass, but they didn't realize I was driven by fear for my health, finances, and housing that I just couldn't stop.

* * *

The empowerment I felt as I improved my health began to spark positive changes in other areas of my life. I was driven to make bold moves, feeling that I had lost so much time, energy, and resources. I wanted to return to college, explore new places, maintain a healthy lifestyle, and achieve financial freedom—most importantly, I never wanted to live in fear again. However, as I rediscovered this new version of myself, it unintentionally caused a growing distance between my then-husband and me. Looking back, I see how this contributed to some poor choices on my part, including being unfaithful—a decision I deeply regret. Ultimately, I made the choice to end the relationship to ensure neither of us got stuck people-pleasing each other for life.

By 2020, I'd finally crossed the finish line. The surgeries were done, and I was free to start living the life I had fought so hard to reclaim. That's when I turned my focus outward. I had spent so many years learning about wellness and perseverance, and I didn't want anyone else to feel as lost and hopeless as I had.

That's what led me to coaching. I wanted to share everything I'd learned and help others take charge of their health and their lives. I dove headfirst into certifications, starting with the Health Coach Institute and then expanding into mastery programs and additional credentials.

This journey wasn't just about transforming my own life; it was about empowering others to do the same. Coaching became my way of turning all the pain, frustration, and lessons into something meaningful. Every client I work with is a reminder of how far I've come—and how much further I can go.

* * *

I began my journey by giving back to the video game community and supporting young gamers, a passion I still hold close to my heart. However, I realized my true calling was in creating a lasting impact through a non-profit, rather than focusing on scaling it for personal gain.

Blending my coaching credentials in health and wellness with my background in art, digital marketing, and web design is where I truly found my stride. This combination has allowed me to craft a unique approach as a Brand Coach, and I'm excited to start working with every client I sign.

This fusion empowers me to guide entrepreneurs in both their personal growth and in building an authentic, powerful brand identity. By merging creativity, strategy, and a holistic approach, I help starry-eyed entrepreneurs set the stage for long-term success in their business and life.

* * *

When I'm not working, I'm dreaming up new visions, goals, and plans for my own life. The list is long, and I'm excited for every single item on it—from the big milestones like bringing this project to life, to the smaller moments like choosing the perfect paint color for our future bedroom. There's nothing I'm not excited about.

Remember those friends I made through gaming as a teen? Well, I reconnected with one throughout my wellness journey, and after knowing each other since 2008, we're now married. Together, we're building a relationship that breaks the mold of what we saw growing up. There's mutual respect, with no attempts to change each other. We set real, non-manipulative boundaries, work on improving intimacy, and address conflict with openness, not avoidance. We've read self-development books, gone to therapy, cried together, and supported each other through challenges, all while maintaining compassion for each other's vulnerabilities.

We've seen too many people approach love in a non-loving way, and that's not what we're here for. We're building a life we love and will protect it from anything negative that slides up back. This is a true partnership, not one born of convenience or codependency. We've learned to pick up the slack when needed, but we prefer to move through life side by side, genuinely enjoying each other's company attached at the hip.

* * *

There are so many other endeavors I want to touch on, it's insane. At the same time, I've rocked my hustle and also enjoy relaxing a bit more, so I look forward to a new phase of balance. Maybe an awesome new project gets released once a year, while I continue to enjoy taking the winter off from client work to sharpen my skills and check in on our dreams. With less survival instinct, I look forward to a more laid-back vibe and nurturing what I've built with less stress.

Did I mention we moonlight as a traveling petsitter duo? Long story short, we care for other people's homes and animals while they go away on long trips. It's been a fantastic way to catch up on savings, meet new people, and travel to areas we never thought we'd see. As animal lovers and previous fosters, we've toyed with the idea of creating an animal sanctuary. That one's a big dream, and likely many years off. Perhaps our retirement dream?

A project even closer to my heart is finally following through on developing an indie video game. Combining my love for storytelling and game mechanics, I'm working on a concept that will provide a fun and meaningful experience for players. It's an ongoing journey, but I'm excited every day to be able to create something that merges my creativity with my technical skills. That one's medium and probably about five years off.

On the horizon, I have ambitious goals to expand my business, collaborate with more like-minded entrepreneurs, and continue to grow in my role as a coach and mentor. I'm looking to host brand retreats and dream of a future live event for *The Girl on the Left*, where everyone in this book can speak in person and guide us through cool experiences with their unique skills and specializations.

This project scared the fuck out of me. It's the first time I've been in a leadership position facilitating this many people, and there was so much unseen pressure to have each milestone tied to this go off without a hitch (spoilers: there were some hitches). Each chapter in this book is an amazing story and voice that was vulnerable enough to step forward and trust me with their words. The more I met these incredible women and heard their stories, the more I was determined to not have this project fail.

I can guarantee you that without the responsibility of other voices being involved, I would not be releasing a book in any capacity. It would end up procrastinating and thrown into my graveyard of dead creative plans, maybe to be revisited in ten years.

There is never a good time to do the thing you're scared to do. Just get it out of the way and start doing it anyway before you steal more time and power from yourself.

The young girl in my story? I didn't want to associate with her for the longest time. I didn't have any love for her. To me, she was weak, a repeated failure, and someone who just couldn't figure it out and get her shit together. Those aren't things I identify with now, so I didn't want to identify with her and accept her as a part of me. That being said, I had to have my epiphany at some point and realize she was the one who made it happen. She did all the digging around, all the trial and error, and paved the way for me to still be here today thriving. So, cheers to our past selves, as I've realized they deserve far more love and acceptance than they're typically credited.

SCAN TO MEET MEGAN

# MARY BOURAS

## INFERTILITY, PURPOSE & TWINS

When I met Pete, I knew nothing about the military. In fact, I had assumed that joining the military was for people who had no other options. But as we began our life together, I quickly realized how wrong I was. Pete's commitment and the realities of military life showed me a whole new world that required sacrifices and resilience I never expected.

In the early years of dating and our marriage, I had a clear sense of who I was and where I was going. I had my own career, my own ambitions, and a life that was independent from Pete's military role. But with each move, it became harder to hold onto that version of myself. I found myself constantly starting over—new jobs, new friends, new routines. I'll confess: The military life threw curveballs my way—fleeting friendships that lasted shorter than a Netflix series, constant chaos, and loneliness that seeped into your bones. While Pete's career soared, mine stalled. I gave up my career to follow him from one duty station to the next, and each time, I felt a little piece of myself slipping away.

At some point, my identity became tied to his—to his career, his achievements, and even his social security number. I was no longer "Mary"; I was "Pete's wife," a title that came with its own set of expectations within the military community. I felt the pressure to fit into a mold—raising a family, being the supportive spouse, and keeping everything together on the home front while Pete served. It seemed like everywhere I turned, other military wives were starting families, and I began to feel like I was falling behind, not just in my career, but in life.

Infertility. It's a word that carries so much weight, especially in a community where families are often seen as a reflection of stability and success. For Pete and me, our journey to parenthood began with so much hope. We were living in Hawaii, enjoying our second Navy tour, and eager to start a family. We had been married for three years. Both our families were back in St. Louis, and I couldn't wait to share the news of the pregnancy with them. I imagined the excitement in my mom's voice when I'd tell her she was going to be a Yiayia (grandmother in Greek) and how Pete's family would celebrate our little miracle. But as the months passed and my body remained stubbornly empty, that hope began to dim, and the joy I imagined turned into quiet sorrow.

On top of dealing with infertility, I found myself grappling with the identity shift that comes with being a military spouse. Moving from place to place, uprooting my career, and leaving behind friends and family left me feeling isolated. I had always been a driven and independent woman, but as the months of trying to conceive went on, I realized I had lost sight of who I was outside of Pete's career and our journey to parenthood. It's not something we talk about often, but as military spouses, we sacrifice a lot more than just stability—we sacrifice pieces of ourselves.

After six months of trying, I took action. I wasn't the type to sit back and wait for life to happen to me. I've always been someone who faces challenges head-on, and this felt no different. I went to the military clinic, and they ran a battery of tests. The diagnosis: unexplained infertility. It was a label that provided no answers, only more questions. I was 30 years old, in the prime of my life, and yet, something as natural as conceiving a child was proving impossible.

That diagnosis, "unexplained infertility," felt like a betrayal. I couldn't help but wonder if my body had failed me. My family's history didn't help ease my worries. My father's side had its share of infertility struggles, and I began to believe I might be doomed to follow the same path. Was I somehow unworthy of this? What did this say about me as a woman? The thoughts were relentless, and they chipped away at my confidence.

As the wife of a military officer, I felt an unspoken pressure to fit into a certain mold. In the military world, family is everything, and for many women, that means children. I couldn't help but feel like I was letting Pete down, like I wasn't fulfilling my role as both his wife and a military spouse. We moved from base to base, and while my husband's career continued to thrive, I was left feeling stagnant—unable to find my own identity amid the chaos. Not only was I struggling to conceive, but I was also struggling to find myself.

But I wasn't about to give up without a fight. Desperation pushed me to try anything and everything that might increase our chances. We tried Clomid for several months with no success. I scoured forums, blogs, and books, seeking miracle cures. I even resorted to using egg whites as a makeshift fertility aid—a tactic that, looking back, seems absurd. But in those moments, when hope is slipping through your fingers, you grasp at anything that offers the slightest glimmer of a chance.

When the doctors suggested we try IUI (intrauterine insemination) or IVF (in vitro fertilization), I knew I couldn't wait any longer. We jumped straight into IVF. By this time, we had relocated to England. The clinic we chose had a reputation for success—it was started by the doctor who performed the first-ever successful IVF. I was convinced this was it; this was our answer.

IVF is not only emotionally taxing but financially draining. Military salaries aren't exactly generous, and the price of a round of IVF felt daunting. Thankfully, the clinic offered a program where you could receive IVF for free if you donated half of your eggs. It seemed like a win-win: we could save money and potentially help another couple conceive. I went through the rigorous process of daily injections, hormonal mood swings, and egg retrieval. The physical pain was bearable, but the emotional toll—it's something no one can prepare you for.

When the procedure was over, I had produced 22 eggs—11 for us, and 11 for the other couple. The sense of responsibility weighed heavy on me. These were more than just cells; they represented our hopes, our future. How could I not get pregnant with 11 eggs? Days later, two embryos were transferred back inside me, and then came the longest two weeks of my life. Every twinge, every flutter, every little sensation had me convinced it worked. But when I started bleeding the night before the blood test, I knew it was over.

I wasn't pregnant. I was devastated. That moment in the shower, digging the progesterone out of me—it's etched into my memory. It felt like I was trying to physically remove the failure, the shame. And to make matters worse, the clinic informed us that the other couple didn't get pregnant either. My eggs weren't viable for donation, which meant we were kicked out of the donor program. The guilt was overwhelming. I had failed not only myself but another couple who had placed their hopes in my body.

For the first time in my life, I couldn't succeed, no matter how hard I tried. I had always prided myself on being able to overcome any challenge, but this—this was different. I felt like I was failing at the most fundamental duty of being a woman, and the depression was suffocating. Every announcement of a friend's pregnancy felt like a personal blow. My body had betrayed me, and I couldn't escape the constant reminder of what I lacked.

Around this time, a story emerged of a transgender woman, transitioning to male, who decided to halt the process to become pregnant—and succeeded. I was infuriated. It felt like a cruel twist of fate that someone who actively chose to change their sex could conceive, while I, who so desperately wanted a child, could not. The unfairness of it all deepened my despair and sense of failure, as though life was playing a game I couldn't win.

Pete, ever supportive, encouraged me to refocus. He reminded me of my love for event management, of the career I had been passionate about before this struggle had consumed me. That's when he told me about the Protocol Office in the military—a perfect blend of event planning and military structure. It was an opportunity to channel my energy and redefine my identity outside of my infertility.

I pitched the idea of an unpaid internship in the Protocol Office to the base commander in England. I offered to work full-time for six months in exchange for a recommendation to Andrews AFB in D.C., home of Air Force One. To my surprise, they agreed. The work was intense, but it was exactly what I needed—a distraction, a purpose, a way to feel like "me" again. By the end of my internship, I had earned the trust of high-ranking officials. One general was so impressed with my work that he personally called the base commander in D.C. to recommend me for a position.

When we moved to D.C., I continued volunteering until the hiring process was finalized. My work in Protocol was nothing short of amazing. I was meeting world leaders and senior cabinet members, and I had the incredible opportunity to introduce my mom to President Obama. It was a moment she could never have imagined in her wildest dreams, especially considering she immigrated from Greece at 16, speaking no English. In those moments, I began to see that life wasn't just about one path. While motherhood eluded me, my career blossomed in ways I never expected.

And yet, even as I threw myself into my career, the dream of motherhood never left me. We decided to try IVF again, this time at Walter Reed Medical Facility in D.C. The costs were more manageable compared to IVF in the civilian sector, but the emotional toll was still staggering. The process was grueling, with four shots a day to my stomach. The egg retrieval resulted in 11 eggs, and when only two embryos survived, I tried to prepare myself for the worst. But no amount of preparation could soften the heartbreak when, once again, I started bleeding before the pregnancy test. I felt like a failure all over again. The familiar waves of self-loathing and hopelessness hit me hard.

We decided on one last round. This was it—our last shot. I was exhausted, physically, emotionally, and financially drained. When I woke up from the egg retrieval, the news wasn't good. Only seven eggs this time. My heart sank. It felt like the universe was conspiring against me, daring me to quit.

But then, the call came. Three embryos had survived, and two were viable. We transferred all three. This time, I tried to busy myself with work to distract from the waiting, but the fear never left me. Finally, the day came for the blood test. I stood outside the airplane hangar during a retirement ceremony, my phone in hand, my heart racing. Then, the message from Walter Reed: "Congratulations, Mary, your beta test is positive."

I was pregnant. In that moment, the darkness that had hung over me for so long lifted. Two weeks later, an ultrasound confirmed it—twins.

My baby girls were born healthy, strong, and perfect. The journey to get to them was anything but easy, but looking back, I wouldn't change a thing. Had I gotten pregnant right away, I would have missed out on the most incredible work experience of my life. The lessons I learned in resilience, in pivoting, and in thinking outside the box are lessons I carry with me today as a coach.

## LESSONS LEARNED: BUILDING STRENGTH THROUGH SETBACKS

Infertility taught me some of the hardest lessons I've ever had to learn, but they have also been the most transformative. I've always been someone who tackles challenges head-on and pushes through to success. However, infertility was different. No amount of planning, perseverance, or hard work could guarantee the result I wanted so badly. That realization was humbling, even paralyzing at times.

### RESILIENCE THROUGH REJECTION

Through each failed IVF round, I felt myself confronting the reality that some things are simply beyond my control. Learning to accept rejection—both from my own body and from the medical system that couldn't offer guarantees—was like being thrown into a crash course on resilience. I learned that failure doesn't define me, but how I respond to it does. This was a pivotal lesson, one that I now pass on to my coaching clients. We are so often conditioned to view setbacks as dead ends, but they're really just detours, forcing us to grow in ways we never imagined. My journey didn't just make me resilient; it made me someone who understands how to bounce back from life's most brutal blows.

### RECLAIMING CONTROL IN A CHAOTIC TIME

When Pete encouraged me to refocus on my career, I initially felt like it was a distraction from my goal of becoming a mother. But as I threw myself into the Protocol Office and eventually landed that dream job at Andrews AFB, I realized something vital: I was still capable of making an impact, even if my original dreams weren't coming to fruition. I regained a sense of purpose, and that became a critical turning point for me emotionally. I learned that, in times of uncertainty, reclaiming even small elements of control can be incredibly empowering. This is a lesson I now emphasize in my coaching—sometimes, it's not about changing the goal but about finding a new path toward fulfillment.

## EMPATHY FOR OTHERS

The emotional isolation that came with infertility was profound. Well-meaning friends and family often said things that unintentionally hurt, suggesting surrogacy or adoption as if those were easy or obvious choices. Going through this experience gave me an unparalleled level of empathy. I know how it feels to have your pain minimized or misunderstood. As a coach, this lesson taught me to meet women where they are, to listen deeply, and to never assume that someone's journey should look a certain way. Sometimes, the most healing thing we can do for another person is simply acknowledge that their pain is real and valid.

## EMBRACING THE "WHY NOT" MINDSET

One of the most powerful lessons I learned throughout my infertility journey—and my life as a military spouse—was to embrace the "why not" mindset. This perspective has opened doors to incredible opportunities I never thought possible. Why not be a featured extra in a Hollywood movie like *You, Me and Dupree*? Why not seek out a private audience with the Patriarch of the Greek Orthodox Church in Istanbul, akin to having a meeting with the Pope? I realized that saying "why not" to life's possibilities transformed my approach to challenges. Rather than letting fear or doubt hold me back, I learned to take bold steps, pursue passions, and seize opportunities that seemed out of reach. This mindset has not only empowered me to tackle obstacles but has also become a fundamental part of my identity. Now, I encourage other women to embrace their own "why not" moments, because it's in those leaps of faith that we often find our most rewarding experiences.

## THE POWER OF PIVOTING

Alongside the "why not" mindset, one of the most significant lessons I took away from this experience was the power of the pivot. Much like Ross from *Friends*, screaming "Pivot!" while struggling to move a couch up the stairs, I had to shift directions—only my couch was my life plan. My entire world had been centered around the idea of becoming a mother, and when that didn't happen easily, I had to ask myself, "What now?" Infertility forced me to redefine what success and fulfillment looked like. By stepping into the world of military protocol and event planning, I discovered talents and passions I hadn't fully realized before. This wasn't giving up—it was expanding. I still wanted to be a mother, but in the meantime, I found purpose in building a career and developing skills that would serve me in all areas of life.

Looking back, the path to motherhood wasn't at all what I expected, but it shaped me into who I am today. Navigating the complexities of infertility while feeling lost in my identity as a military spouse forced me to confront the question of who I was beyond the roles I played. It taught me that life doesn't always go according to plan, but it's in those moments of uncertainty and heartache that we discover our true strength. I learned to embrace resilience, to pivot when life demands it, and to find purpose beyond failure. Today, as I watch my twin daughters grow into strong, confident young women, I'm reminded that even the hardest journeys can lead to the most beautiful destinations. My experiences as a military spouse and my struggles with infertility have fueled my passion to help other women navigate their own challenges. I understand, all too well, that within every struggle lies the potential for growth, healing, and unshakable confidence.

SCAN TO MEET MARY

# TAYLER MCCOLLUM

## BULLYING, BRAVERY & TRUE BEAUTY

Hey, I'm Tayler Jade, and here's my story.

I was born with a cleft lip and palate. I'm deaf in my left ear and blind in my right eye, and I have had 20-plus surgeries from when I was a baby to 18 years old.

I was bullied when I was younger, and I hated the way I looked through middle school and some in high school. I still look at the scars I have. I'm so insecure about them, and of course, I tell myself that they are just scars. Every time I had surgery, I would pray because I was so scared, but I knew deep down that everything was gonna be okay.

We are all different, quirky, and weird. But honestly? Who cares because that uniqueness is what makes us all special, worth getting to know, and one of a kind.

You know, in truth, being bullied only made me stronger, and it made me realize that I have a voice and that I need to use my voice to speak up and say something about being bullied and about being worried about what someone else says about me.

In some ways, I'm glad it happened to me because, truthfully, it just made me feel stronger, braver, and able to speak up and hopefully help others.

I really want to be able to go through life knowing that I'm making not only a difference in my life but also in someone else's life. I didn't smile so much growing up, only if someone made me smile and then made me feel good about myself, but sometimes that wasn't always the case.

You know, I am really glad that I'm sharing this because it's not good holding something in like that; it's really better to say something.

For so long, I felt so alone growing up, nobody knew how upset, angry, and scared I was. I felt like I was going through this by myself, even though I wasn't. I had family and friends who knew that I had surgeries and who would send me texts and call me.

I have never had so much love and kind words from them and also the doctors and nurses who helped me so much. I wish that I could turn back and just say thank you. I mean, I did when I was in recovery, but I just want to say thank you again.

When I was growing up, it was hard for me, being the girl that was different, being blind in one eye and wearing glasses and being deaf in one ear and having to wear hearing aids. The whole experience was a lot.

I felt so insecure about the way I looked, but it took me some time, and then I realized that it didn't matter what was on the outside, but the inside was important. So many had told me that, and I had a hard time believing and seeing that, but I have seen it. I also learned that no matter what I went through as a little kid, other people are going through, too.

When I was going through my surgeries, I used to think I wasn't strong enough, that I was just weak, but I actually just looked in the mirror one day, and I told myself that I was strong. I would write notes and write on a little whiteboard and told myself I was, and I even wrote some of my quotes like "Never let the fear of striking out keep you from playing the game" and "Nothing is impossible, even the word itself says I'm possible."

Every day, I would say those words to myself. I really didn't like my scars growing up. I thought that they were horrible and ugly, but as I grew up, I understood even more that they were part of who I am. I knew then I couldn't change myself to fit someone else's idea of me because, at the end of the day, I had to just tell myself that I was brave and that I could overcome any obstacles, big or small.

When I was being bullied, I would see what others saw, and I would be so depressed: I hated myself, I hated the way I looked.

But one day, I just looked in the mirror, and I just told myself that I wasn't gonna let others make me feel ugly, dumb, or make me feel about bad about myself. I mean, I can't change what I went through, but I can change how I feel about myself. So, I held my chin up high, and it was still hard for me at times, but as time went on, I decided not to let any more comments, looks, and fingers pointed get to me. I did lose friends, well, those who I thought were my friends and, yes, it did hurt, but it didn't break me into a million pieces.

It just made me realize who my real friends are and who I can really trust. I didn't let people in because I didn't want them to feel sorry for me or to feel like they are obligated to hang out with me or talk to me. I hate that there are people who are getting bullied, and they probably feel like they can't talk to anybody; that's not true, they do have people to talk to and who can help.

Having a cleft lip and palate, and being deaf in one ear and blind in one eye was and still is hard. I have had over 20 surgeries between birth and turning 18 years old. I can't change being blind in one eye and deaf in one ear. I am sure that there are others who have a cleft lip and palate who are going through the same thing as me, but if they are, they are not alone.

For those who are being bullied, I want you to know that you're not alone and that those who are bullying you are just jealous and insecure about themselves that they wanna make you feel unhappy and ugly about yourself, but you shouldn't let anybody tell you anything different. You are all beautiful and handsome.

God made you who you are. God made me the way I am, and he made each and every one of you the way you are. If life gets hard, just know that you do have people on your side that you can talk to. I felt like I was a freak growing up, and I think in my mind, that's what I thought everyone else saw me as, but they didn't.

They just saw me as a girl who is strong and who is going through a lot, and she'll continue to go through a lot.

Being bullied just made me stronger, and it made me realize that I shouldn't let some comments bring me down because of my nose or my lip. I can't change what happened, and if you are going through the same thing as me, you are not alone.

See that beautiful sunset outside?

I love looking at it because it makes the biggest thing feel small. I mean, I really thought I was alone, but then I had to learn that I'm not alone and neither are you or anybody else.

Being in the hospital can do a lot to a kid. You're missing out on things you can be doing, but you have to take it easy. Nobody really understood how hard it was for me, surgery after surgery, not being able to sleep because of the monitors, but in the end, it all worked out in the long run.

It took me a while to find myself again, not the old me but this new me because after the bullying had stopped for a while, it took me some time to find myself again. Being bullied had changed me, it made me feel less than and lost, but I had people in my corner who helped me see that I was more, that I was a good sweet person who deserves to live life and to always stay strong and brave.

It was hard to trust and to find my new friends and people who weren't looking at me like I was ugly. I was feeling depressed, and I would cry and just keep to myself, which didn't help at all. Being bullied made me feel less than, and it changed me. I needed to open up and talk to others honestly.

I didn't want to feel like that again—I wanted to say something, I wanted to speak up and make some changes and try to find something that I could use to get my words and message across.

That's why I made my blog to write what I couldn't say and my podcast to speak what I wanted to get off my chest. Having both has really helped me and is continuing to help me get out of my shell.

I changed schools when I was in the 8th grade. I went to a new school, and I was the new girl in some way. I didn't think I would make friends because I was the new girl. I came in the middle of the school year; it was rough for me during that time because you are trying to find your place in school with people who are already friends. I found my friends, old and new, and I even got more bullies, too, but it wasn't as bad as it was before.

I'm still friends with wonderful people since it was so different from my old school. I wasn't wearing uniforms, which was a plus.

I really had some challenges through school, but I made it through. What's so hard about school is the technology and how it can be easy for people to bully others and find ways to spread rumors and hate.

Cyberbullying is absolutely scary, and I really feel like the teachers and principals need to be more aware and more strict when it comes to phones and computers because anybody can post something or text something, and that can hurt people and mess with their mental health.

For me, I didn't use my phone so much, and I only used a computer for school stuff. I have never had someone do anything to me online at school, but it can happen, and things need to change about that.

School is supposed to be a learning experience, to meet and hang out with friends, to try out for school activities; it's not supposed to be a place for anybody to get bullied or hurt.

I just hope that me talking about being bullied, and about seeing who your friends are, and seeing how life can change you, is helpful to someone.

Being bullied shouldn't happen, but it does. Sadly, it happens more often than you would think. Like I said, I think that when I was being bullied, it changed me, it made me stronger than I once was, and it made me realize that I had to find myself and that I needed to figure out what I wanted for myself and for my life.

I didn't want to go around and see what people thought of me, I didn't wanna hear the whispers, which I always knew there were some, and I knew that people would think I was ugly, not pretty enough, or that I wasn't good enough. I truly had to change my point of view and see that life is scary, but as long as you have people around you to help you, it does get better, it just takes time for that to happen.

So, I have had so many issues with loving myself because it can be too hard to love yourself, to feel good about yourself, to be happy with yourself and the way you look, and also the way others look at you, but here's the thing: Nobody can tell you how to be you, how to love yourself, how to feel good about yourself—the only person that can do that is you. I know what it is like to not love yourself, or care about yourself, but over time, I have been learning that I need to love myself more, that I need to love others. I need to believe in myself and not doubt myself, which can be really hard, but I encourage you to do the same.

You shouldn't be hard on yourself, because you are amazing, even if you don't believe that in yourself or see it the way you are. I'm sure others feel the same way about you.

When I think about the "what ifs," they didn't help me at all. I would say, "What if I'm not beautiful, what if I'm not smart enough, what if I'm not strong enough?" Saying those things was negative in my life, I was so taking that to heart, and I was putting that into my head, and I went on thinking that about me and about my life. I knew that from experience about hating myself and not caring, but I needed to open my eyes and realize that I was only hurting myself.

I caused harm to myself emotionally, spiritually, and to my mental health. I would body shame myself by saying that I was ugly. I honestly was taking in what people were saying to me, that I wasn't beautiful, that I was ugly, dumb, not worthy. Those words I took to heart, but then I grew, and I'm still learning as a young adult, I'm still learning to love myself. If you are also still learning to love yourself, then you will get there.

You just have to keep going because the person inside and outside is amazing and extraordinary.

The point that I hope to make and I hope to help someone else is that you have to look at yourself in the mirror and tell yourself that you are beautiful, worthy, and lovely. You just need to say positive words. You can do something that makes you feel good about yourself because, trust me, there are things that you can do to make you feel great. Growing up as a kid and then going into my teens, I really had to learn to love myself and do things that made me feel good.

You need to find something that makes you feel really good about yourself because that's all that matters.

Loving yourself, taking care of yourself, and being yourself is all that matters.

Nobody can tell you how to take care of yourself, you have to do that yourself because, honestly, not taking care of yourself can hurt you in a way you may not even know it. It can mess with your mental health and your physical, emotional, and spiritual health.

For the past few years, I have truly struggled with taking compliments. I mean, everyone tells me such sweet and nice things, but it's like I can't take them, and I pass them off to them and say the things they say to me. I don't do it to say that I don't deserve it, but I just don't feel it, and I know I need to work on that.

I know that it's hard for me to accept those compliments sometimes because I didn't get those compliments a lot growing up. I got more of the negative than the positive ones, but as I got to my teens and now young adult, I'm still working on accepting those compliments, and I even write them down and put them on my walls or mirrors as a reminder to always tell myself that.

Having some self-confidence and affirmations for myself helps, and I hope it helps you as well if you do it too.

You know, growing up, I wanted to be so many things.

I wanted to be a lawyer, CSI, or psychologist, but honestly, I think motivational speaker is what I want to do because I love using my voice to speak up, and I want to help others who are dealing with being bullied, dealing with having a cleft lip and palate, having so many surgeries and who are feeling like they don't matter.

I know it sounds crazy, but I'm just doing small videos on TikTok, Instagram, and Facebook, talking about my story and doing my podcast and blog. I'm trying to spread positivity on those platforms. That's what I'm trying to do, what my goal is, and what I hope to reach and accomplish.

I don't know if I can even reach a room full of people or friends online and offline, but if I can even reach one or five, then that'll be enough for me, at least I'm doing something to help others.

I have struggled with having friends growing up, now, I do have my friends from school and my childhood that I still talk to, but these past few months, I have met some amazing people on TikTok who have really become some of my closest friends. I know we haven't met in person but talking to them every day and getting to know them on TikTok and off TikTok, I have gotten to know them as an amazing, wonderful, and extraordinary group of people.

It's rare to find those friends on platforms and to still have some good friends from childhood and from school, it's really hard to find those good friends who support you, be there for you to lean on, to vent to.

You can never have too many friends, but at the end of the day, it's all about those who will respect you and who won't hurt you or judge you or what you've been through, even if it's just 1, 5, or 20 closest friends, that's pretty amazing.

I hope you all have those close friends you care about and who care about you.

**SCAN TO MEET TAYLER**

# SAMANTHA BAILEY

## INFIDELITY, DECEPTION & BETRAYAL TRAUMA

I was born and raised in Canada, where my childhood was shaped by the values of family, resilience, and a strong sense of community. Growing up, I was surrounded by the landscapes of my homeland—the tall pines, snowy winters, and lakes that sparkled in the summer sun. Life there was a blend of tradition and love, grounded in family bonds that taught me early on the importance of support and care for one another.

In my family, caring for others was second nature, and it became a core part of who I was. Those values would follow me wherever I went, becoming the foundation of my life.

In the early 1990s, I moved to Texas and found myself in a completely new environment, one filled with different landscapes and warmer winters but, ultimately, similar values. Texas was a place where family, loyalty, and community were celebrated, and it didn't take long for it to feel like home. I embraced the new culture, and over time, Texas became my world, the place where my dreams, my family, and my life would unfold.

Here, I became a mother to six incredible children who became the center of my universe. Raising my family in Texas was both a joy and a journey. Each of my children brought unique challenges and gifts, and they taught me so much about resilience, love, and the endless capacity of the heart to nurture and care.

Being a mother was everything to me, and later, becoming a grandmother brought even more joy into my life. My family became my anchor, the foundation upon which I built my identity and purpose. Nurturing others was at the heart of who I was, and this carried over into my career as well. I was drawn to roles that allowed me to support and help others, gravitating toward professions where I could make a difference, be it through listening, guiding, or simply being a source of comfort in difficult times.

I found fulfillment in service, knowing that I was making a small but meaningful impact on the lives of those around me. My life's work was about giving—whether at home with my children or in my professional life, my focus was always on helping others feel seen, understood, and cared for.

But life, as I would come to learn, has its own plans, and sometimes they lead us down roads we could never have anticipated. For years, I believed my life was on a steady path. I had built a family, a career, and a life rooted in stability and trust. My marriage, too, was something I relied on, a partnership that I thought was grounded in mutual respect, loyalty, and love. I never questioned the trust I had in my husband.

To me, our marriage was a safe harbor, a place of companionship and shared history. Little did I know that beneath the surface, there was another story waiting to be revealed, a truth that would shake the very foundation of my world.

The discovery was as unexpected as it was devastating. It came on an ordinary day, one that began like any other, without warning of the emotional storm that was about to break. I stumbled upon evidence that pointed to a hidden life, one my husband had kept secret from me for years. At first, I couldn't believe what I was seeing. It was as if I were looking at a story that belonged to someone else, something distant and unreal. But as the pieces started to come together, the reality became undeniable. My husband, the man I had trusted implicitly, had been living a life filled with deceit and betrayal.

I uncovered details that I could hardly comprehend. My husband had been involved with sugar babies, escorts, and numerous affairs—a secret world that shattered the image I had of our life together. The betrayal was all-encompassing; it wasn't just about the physical acts of infidelity but about the lies, the hidden life, and the realization that the man I thought I knew was, in some ways, a stranger. The revelation felt like a physical blow, a pain so deep it seemed to reach into the core of my being. I felt as though my entire life had collapsed, that everything I had believed in had been built on a foundation of lies.

In those initial moments, I was overwhelmed by a wave of emotions that left me feeling hollow and numb. There was shock, a disorienting disbelief that made it difficult to process the reality of the situation. Anger followed, a fiery rage that burned through the numbness, filling me with a sense of betrayal that was almost unbearable. And then came the sadness, a deep, soul-crushing grief for the life I thought I had, for the marriage I believed was real, and for the years that now felt wasted and lost.

The loneliness was overwhelming.

Even though I was surrounded by family and friends who loved me, I felt isolated, trapped in a world of pain that no one else could truly understand. The betrayal wasn't just about my husband's actions; it was about a fundamental breach of trust, one that shook my belief in myself and in the world around me.

I found myself questioning everything—my judgment, my worth, and even my ability to trust others. I had spent so much of my life giving to others, caring for my family, and building a life based on love and loyalty. Now, I was left with nothing but questions and a hollow feeling of betrayal that seemed impossible to fill. I felt as though I had lost not only my marriage but a part of myself.

The woman I was, the one who trusted, who believed in the goodness of those she loved, was gone, replaced by someone who was broken, hurt, and desperately searching for answers.

In those dark days following the discovery, I felt like I was drowning in a sea of emotions that I couldn't control. The pain was so intense that it felt like a physical presence, an ache that settled deep in my chest and refused to leave. I knew I needed to find a way to cope, a way to release some of the overwhelming feelings that threatened to consume me. That was when I turned to journaling, almost on a whim, as a means to express the pain that words couldn't seem to capture.

Writing became my sanctuary. Each page was a place where I could pour out the turmoil inside me, where I could give voice to the grief, anger, and confusion that I felt trapped within. At first, my entries were raw and unfiltered, a stream of emotions that seemed too intense to contain. I wrote about the pain of betrayal, the anger at being deceived, and the heartbreak of losing the life I thought I had. The pages became a mirror for my soul, a place where I could see my pain reflected back at me, raw and unfiltered.

Over time, though, something began to shift. What started as an outlet for my pain began to evolve into something more—a path toward healing. Through writing, I found a way to process the trauma, to make sense of the chaos that had taken over my life. Journaling allowed me to step back and look at my pain from a distance, to see it as a part of my story but not the whole of it. It became a way to reclaim my voice, to assert my identity in a world that had been turned upside down.

The betrayal not only fractured my marriage but shattered my sense of identity. Trust had been such a core part of who I was, and I had built my life around the belief that people—especially those closest to me—were fundamentally good and honest. When that trust was broken, it felt as though my understanding of the world had changed entirely.

I began to question everything I knew about myself, my decisions, and the choices I had made over the years. How could I have missed this? I asked myself that question repeatedly, grappling with the fear that perhaps I hadn't been as strong or as aware as I had believed.

This kind of betrayal goes beyond the immediate pain; it creates a ripple effect that touches every part of life. I became more guarded, cautious, and fearful. The openness and trust that had once defined me now felt like vulnerabilities I needed to protect. I realized that betrayal trauma wasn't just about the acts themselves; it was about the way those acts undermined my very sense of self.

I found myself withdrawing from relationships and questioning the intentions of others, even those who had never given me a reason to doubt them. I wondered if I could ever trust again, not just others but also my own judgment.

This uncertainty and self-doubt took a toll on my mental health. There were nights when I lay awake, replaying every moment, every conversation, and every memory that now felt tainted by the lies I had uncovered. I questioned my past, my choices, and even the love I had once felt. Was it real? Had I been blind to signs that others might have seen? These thoughts were relentless, a cycle of questioning that seemed to have no end. In those moments, it felt as though I was losing myself, piece by piece, to a darkness that I couldn't escape.

As time passed, I realized that if I were to find peace, I would have to rebuild my life from the ground up. The pieces of who I once was lay scattered, and it was up to me to decide which ones were worth keeping and which needed to be left behind. I began to see this journey as an opportunity not just to heal, but to redefine who I was and what I wanted for my life.

This wasn't an easy realization.

In fact, it was terrifying.

But deep down, I knew that my story didn't have to end with betrayal. It could become a story of resilience, strength, and transformation.

One of the first steps in this journey was to find a support system that could help me navigate the path forward. Although I had always been someone others leaned on, it was now my turn to reach out for help. Therapy became a crucial part of my healing process. Speaking with a therapist allowed me to explore the depths of my pain in a safe, supportive environment. It gave me a space to unpack not just the betrayal itself, but the impact it had on my identity, my sense of worth, and my future.

Through therapy, I learned that healing from betrayal trauma is a journey of reclaiming your power, of finding ways to regain control over your life after it's been thrown into chaos. I started to build new routines, ones that centered on self-care and self-respect. Journaling remained a constant companion, helping me process my emotions and thoughts as they surfaced. Over time, writing became not only a form of expression but a means of self-empowerment. In those pages, I found the courage to set boundaries, to protect my peace, and to prioritize my own well-being.

As I moved forward in my healing journey, I began to feel a new sense of purpose. I realized that the pain I had endured, as isolating as it felt, was not unique to me. There were countless others who had faced betrayal, who had felt the same sense of devastation and loss. I had found a way to cope through journaling and therapy, and it struck me that perhaps my journey could offer others a path to healing as well. I began to write with intention, transforming my private journal entries into something more—a guide, a story, a survival manual for anyone who might be going through a similar experience.

The idea for my book, *Deceptive Liaisons*, was born from this desire to make a difference. I wanted to create something that could provide support, comfort, and guidance to those struggling with the weight of betrayal trauma. Writing the book was not an easy task; it required me to relive painful memories, to dive back into the emotions that I had worked so hard to process. But it was also a cathartic experience. In telling my story, I found a sense of closure, a way to take control of my narrative. The book became a testament to my resilience and a way to offer hope to others.

Through writing, I was able to distill the insights I had gained along the way. I wanted the book to be more than just my story; I wanted it to be a tool for healing. I shared the steps that had helped me find stability in the aftermath of betrayal, emphasizing the importance of self-care, setting boundaries, and allowing oneself the time to grieve. The process of writing and sharing my story became a way to connect with others, to let them know that they were not alone and that healing was possible, even after the deepest betrayals.

As I delved deeper into my healing journey, my desire to help others grew stronger. I had walked through the pain, I had faced the darkness, and I had found a way to survive. Now, I wanted to give back. I decided to pursue training to become a Certified PBT (Post Betrayal Transformation) Coach, a step that would allow me to not only share my story but to actively guide others through their own journeys of recovery. This training gave me the tools and knowledge to understand betrayal trauma on a deeper level, equipping me with the skills to support others in a meaningful and impactful way.

Becoming a coach was more than just a career choice; it was a personal mission. I knew from experience how isolating betrayal trauma could feel, how it could make you question your worth, your choices, and your future. I wanted to be there for others, to offer them the support and guidance I had found in my own journey.

The training process was challenging but fulfilling. I learned about the different stages of betrayal trauma, the emotional and psychological impacts, and the strategies that could help people find their way back to a place of strength and stability.

Through my coaching, I hope to create a safe space for individuals to heal, to rediscover themselves, and to build a life that feels whole once again. My goal is to empower others to reclaim their lives after betrayal, to show them that healing is possible, and to guide them through the process with compassion and empathy. Helping others has always been at the heart of who I am, and now, I am able to do so in a way that is both deeply personal and profoundly impactful.

**SCAN TO MEET SAMANTHA**

# JODI HARTY

## COLLISION, LOSS & PHYSICAL REHABILITATION

Edmonton, Alberta, had just had a massive snowstorm, and roads had been treacherous for days. My four-year-old daughter and I were supposed to be going to see my husband in Fort McMurray, where he worked four hours away. I did not want to go. I was worried about the roads, and to be honest, Mike's and my marriage was not in a good place, and I needed to have a conversation that I knew was not going to be taken well.

I shared with Mike that I did not want to drive on the roads. He assured me that they were fine. He said, "Drive 45 minutes out of the Edmonton area, and the roads were dry and clear." He was not worried.

He was a manager of a trucking company. He was an expert at assessing roads, and he was an expert at assessing my driving capabilities. He assured me the roads were good. He expressed how much he wanted to see me and our daughter Marley.

We had made a promise a few months back to one another, that we both would put in more of an effort in scheduling time to see one another. To put our marriage and our family first. Once a month, he would take time off, and once a month, I would take some time off and go see him. Essentially, we would be seeing each other every two weeks.

I decided to keep the promise I made. To put our marriage first. To put the relationship that he wanted to have with Marley first... To put the relationship that I wanted him to have with Marley first. We were a team, and Mike would never put us in harm's way if it were not safe. He loved his family. He adored Marley and I, and wanted things to be better... Easier.

February 3, 2018, came. I put in a half day of work. Marley was taken swimming and "played out" so that she would mostly sleep on the drive. I picked her up on my way home from work, stopped at our place to pick up a few more items, backed out of the driveway, and called Mike to let him know that we were on our way.

Marley piped up from the back seat and said, "Daddy! Are you so excited to see your *favorite* four-year-old little girl?!?" Marley had three half-sisters, and she *always* made sure not to "discriminate." :) Mike replied, "I sure am, sweetheart." They ended the conversation with how much they loved one another and hung up. Marley was so excited. She was wiggling and giggling with excitement in her car seat.

We had planned a surprise for him. You see, her dad looooved overalls, but she always said they were "for boys." She was a girly girl. Loved frills, laces, dresses, and soft materials. She had a growth spurt recently, so we had gone to buy new clothes and she LOVED a pair of overalls that she found. So, that's what she had decided to wear, Daddy would finally get to see her in overalls.

The next thing I knew, I was leaning to my left over the steering wheel, knowing not to move... I heard a man's voice, and I said, "Call my husband, call my husband." I must have given the man Mike's number because I remember hearing Mike's voice. "Mike?"

"Yes, hunny."
"Is it Saturday?"
"Yes, it is, sweetheart."
"Were we coming to see you?"
"Yes, you were, hunny."

"Mike... I can't hear Marley, I don't know how she is... I can't hear Marley." I remember thinking I should call out to her. A voice inside me said, "She's gone." "QUIET!!!" I yelled in my head. "She's hurt, she's not gone."

That is the last memory that I have of that day. The next thing I remember is being in the ICU, neck collar, hands tied (so I wouldn't try and remove the tubes in confusion), and intubated. They untied my left hand and gave me a pen and paper. I wrote, "Mike, Marley, girls?" I was assured that Mike was there, and the girls were there and okay. I did not get an answer from Marley.

I remember feeling like I was wrapped up in a cocoon. I was very warm, and it felt like I was fully immersed in what looked like warm transparent liquid gold. I could breathe in this fluid, and with each breath, there was a calming, loving feeling. As I was twisting from side to side, upside down and right side up, I was fully immersed in this liquid, I was weightless. I knew something big was happening to me. Nothing hurt. I was just so warm, allowing the current to take me where it wanted. It was like being surrounded by infrared heat all over the body. I was peaceful. I did not want to leave this place... Whatever it was, I wanted to stay there for as long as I could, enjoying the weightlessness, the peace, the calm, the love, and the comfort.

I heard a voice, and it kept saying, "You are going to be fine. You will get through this. You're going to be fine." I don't know how much time had passed, but I knew I was leaving this place. I didn't want to, I was fighting to stay where I was. I wasn't ready to go. I heard the voice, "You are going to be fine, you're going to get through this," fading with that transformative experience... Then came the pain.

With a sudden awareness of my body I woke screaming in pain. Everything was excruciating and bright. I wanted to escape this body that I was in. I wanted to go back to the warm liquid gold. To be wrapped up, weightless... Then it was all black. There was nothing. (Later, years after the collision, I watched the movie *The Impossible* about the Thailand Tsunami. There was a scene where she was underwater, and it was so quiet, as she was tossed around in the water, upright, side to side, she was like an observer but peaceful... THAT was what I felt in the liquid gold. Calm, peace...)

I woke up again, still intubated, still tied, still neck collar. They untied my hand, and this time I wrote. "Dad, sister, Marley." I got all the answers except for Marley. Everything went black again... I woke up a third time, and this time, I wrote. "MARLEY." My family had been pushing for me to get through all my surgeries first to ensure that I did not give up on life. Mike had been advocating that I know...

A mother's heart knows when there is something not right with her children. We are connected at a cellular level... My heart was telling me... My head, on the other hand, was refusing that innate knowledge, and I needed SOMEONE to talk to me. The nurses and doctors did not know HOW I was able to wake myself up. I was supposed to be in a chemically induced coma.

I can tell you that I strived to wake up. I strived to learn about Marley. How she was... Was she still here? Was she hurt? My soul NEEDED this information. My drive as a mother was defying medical science. It was decided that I be told. I remember Mike lovingly sitting beside me. He could not touch me... He could not even rest his hand on my hospital bed because I could feel the vibration of people's breathing through my shattered bones. I do not recall how he started to tell me. What I do remember is, "Marley died in the collision."

"Was it my fault?" I asked.
"NO! Another driver came into your lane and hit you at highway speeds just outside of Grassland." (That was two hours away from home.)
"Was she hurt?" "No, she died instantly on impact."

I do not remember the rest of what was said. I was still heavily sedated. I know that I cried some with Mike. However, I remember thinking, "It will just go back to how it was without her. When I just had Summer and River. It will be like before." (It is not like before.) The 76 milligrams of Dilaudid, anti-psychotics, and ketamine they had me on dulled the feelings.

I knew I should be devastated. I knew I should be sobbing... But I couldn't "feel" much of anything. I was numb. After Mike had told me. I was able to rest. I slept. When I woke again, although I could not even see in front of me due to all the narcotics, it was important that I start seeing a few people.

The first was my girls, Summer and River. I asked if they had touched me yet, and ensured that they had, that they took my hand, that they hugged me if they wanted. It was important for me to reassure them that I was there, that I was going to be fine, not to be scared, and that I was going to get better. I do not remember much of those conversations, but the one question River asked me was, "What do I tell my future kids about their aunt that they will never know?" How does a not-yet 10-year-old girl even begin to process something like that when I, as an adult, didn't even know how to process my own grief? I remember Summer expressing regret and remorse, saying that she could have been a better big sister... A nearly 13-year-old carrying the load regretted that she didn't want to always play with the toddler who wanted to play with Barbies, and dress up... Cliche words of "Hunny, that is normal, and you were the best big sister she could have asked for" didn't even seem to touch the pain that she was in.

Those moments and many after made me feel like I was not a mother. I could not go home with them and grieve with them. I could not hold them, I could not cry with them... All I could do was to lie in that bed not moving, and TRY to reassure them that they would move through this. Others, not me, would be the ones to hold them, dry their tears, and fall asleep with them, ensuring they were surrounded with love... Not me.

They told me I would be in the hospital for 10 months recovering. I told them they were wrong! I had been in the alternative field since 1996, and actively practiced massage therapy for 15 years. I KNEW that it took six weeks for a bone to heal. I argued and said, "I will be walking in six weeks. I've had clients with hip and knee replacements, and they are FINE after six weeks. I only have broken bones... I'm not dumb." No one argued back with me, but I was dumb in hindsight. As much as they explained to me what had been done to me, it did not translate. I couldn't compute it. I couldn't even retain it.

Every day, they told me, and every day, I would forget the severity and just get angry that I wasn't getting better like a normal person. They moved me out of the ICU after a week and into a trauma ward. The hospital agreed to help us so that we could have a small intimate viewing of Marley for goodbyes. We decided to wait for the funeral until I was at least out of the hospital.

I had two weeks from the collision to the time Marley's viewing, to be able to sit up. I had been flat on my back as my nearly snapped-off femoral head could not handle body pressure with its new plate. Every day I practiced sitting up for longer and longer. I wanted to see my daughter. I wanted to hold her hand. Every day I could tolerate longer and longer. On the day of the viewing, the nurses ensured pain meds were not late. I would need a lot in order to get through what was to come. They helped shower me, and my sister had brought my late grandpa's gold and black satin robe for me to wear. In the time that I had been practicing sitting up, I had also been practicing getting in and out of a wheelchair from my bed. In the beginning, it took six people to move me... By the time the viewing came, it only took four.

I remember Mike and I walking into the dimly lit room where Marley was lying. Her hair and makeup were done like she was going to one of her dance recitals. A light pink wool sweater covered her to hide the seatbelt bruising around her neck and shoulder. Mike placed me right beside her, and I instantly went for her hand. He tried to stop me, and I said, "I get to hold my daughter's hand..." It still fit in mine like it did before. She was cold, but she was mine.

I grew that hand, I held that hand when she was sad, or we ran side by side playing. I held that hand when she was sick, when she was scared/nervous as she got onto the preschool bus for swimming lessons, and when she had broken her knee at a trampoline park. I held that hand the day that her dad and I said our wedding vows, and that hand was one of the first things I kissed when I birthed her.

They say a mother's heart beats outside of the body once she has children... I say that is not true. A mother's heart is always connected to her children, and she feels them, but it is ONLY when a child goes onto the other side of the veil, never to be touched again, that a mother's heart also goes with their forever baby... Never to be whole again and always yearning to be reconnected. That day, the power that a mother was shown to everyone who witnessed. That day was the first day that I held Summer and River.

River broke seeing Marley, and I could not get her on me fast enough where she was sitting on my lap. Shattered bones. Titanium rods having been hammered into all my long bones, and only two weeks after the collision, I have an almost 10-year-old and later an almost 13-year-old on my lap as they let out all of their grief of what their life has suddenly become. I should NOT have been able to do that physically or pain-wise.

At the three-week mark, it was then that I started translating that I was NOT going to be walking again in six weeks... That it was more severe than a knee or a hip replacement. That is when I decided that I needed to do everything I could to get out of the hospital faster than 10 months. I had nearly 20 years of experience with the human body, and it was time that I became MY BEST

CLIENT. Implementing EVERYTHING I knew about recovery and how the body heals. Working with chiropractors for the last eight years, I knew that the body heals best in motion. Don't move, don't heal, get sick, die.

So, I moved. I moved from bed to wheelchair, chair to toilet, chair to bed. Physical therapists gave me little 2-lb weights that were insulting to me... but with healing broken ribs, punctured intestine, and kidney, I wasn't allowed to do more than 2 lbs at that time. I practiced wheeling myself down the hallways, and when I got tired, family and friends pushed me, until I was ready again. I did my very best to ensure that the food I ate was healing food that would not cause further body pain and add to inflammation. I did EVERYTHING I WAS TOLD and advocated for more.

I was moved to a rehabilitation hospital, even though I was non-weight bearing, four weeks after the collision as I was transferring so well and only needed two people to help me from wheelchair to bed, etc. There, I began the intense therapies. Psychologists, physical therapy, and occupational therapy for the upper body that I insisted on. I knew that when the time came to stand again, I would need every bit of upper body strength to hold me up so I could at least do the motions of walking to rebuild those neuropathways.

Even if I couldn't put weight on my legs, I could hold myself up and do the movements, which would enable faster recovery. Five days a week. One hour of physical therapy. Followed by one hour of upper body and abdominal strength training. Eight weeks after the collision, I was given pool privileges, and then two times a week, I included pool therapy into this routine for one hour. (People that include pool therapy get better 50% faster.) Add to that one hour of intense therapy to prepare me for a life outside of the hospital and to be a mother to two girls... Not three.

During this time, my husband and I did not fare well. We ended up separating only five weeks after the collision. When you have a collision of this magnitude, every problem is magnified for you, each other, and your close family to see. We were both trying, but we were not kind to one another. I was still on 56 milligrams of opioids, even though I had weaned off of the ketamine. I was still on the antipsychotics and was not able to retain information, track time, or be able to discern HOW I was communicating, but I also could not find different words to communicate better. I was cruel...

He was unable to understand in his own grief and anger. He felt alone and unsupported, and I felt like no matter what, he was not hearing me. Although we loved each other fiercely, it was not felt by either of us. I kicked him out of my room. He understood it to be permanent. I only meant for him to go where he needed to be to receive the support that I could not give him... The damage was too deep and had been done.

I was released after four months of being in the hospital. I could only stand/walk for more than 2 minutes at a time and could do 13 stairs, but I was well enough. I lived with my family and had "visitations on weekends with my girls" until I was strong enough to live on my own three months later after release. I maintained my therapies just like I did in the hospital for the next two years adding rehabilitation TRX and rehabilitation yoga until 2020, when 3/4 of my therapies were deemed nonessential. I lost much of my recovery... but that's another story.

After the first year, I resumed looking after my girls 50% of the time (back to shared custody), and I achieved my certification for Health and Life coaching. I learned to create programs for women who were grieving or going through life changes based on my former education.

I haven't stopped there, though. I continue to speak publicly, and I now am a board-certified hormone and drugless practitioner coach so that I can do comprehensive labs to get to the root cellularly, physically, emotionally, and mentally.

I share my story not for others to feel sad or pity but to know that you can have your whole life ripped away, never to be rebuilt again the same... But you can thrive. You can achieve great things. You can move through hard things. You don't have to stay stuck or feel hopeless.

All you have to do is decide and then begin working with experts who can help you.

Marley will ALWAYS be part of my life. I AM a mother of three, but that is not my identity.

I ask you, who are you without your titles?

When you're not a mother, daughter, sister, aunt. You are not your career or faith, but who you are to your core.

I am strong.
I am perseverant.
I am a healer.
I am a helper.
I am intelligent.
I am powerful.

...AND SO ARE YOU.

Marley has taught me ALL of this since that fateful day, February 3, 2018.

SCAN TO MEET JODI

# KINGSLEY

## AUTHENTICITY, DREAMS & STARDOM

When I look back on my journey, it's all about becoming the person I dreamed of as a kid—the bold, audacious, vivacious girl I didn't see anywhere. Growing up, I felt the absence of her in the world, so I decided to create her myself. That's how Kingsley was born.

It started in sixth grade. My sisters and I had a girl group called *Heartfilled*, and we were choosing stage names. Our mom said, "Pick whatever you want!" My sister Dom went with *Phoenix*, and my sister Bre chose *Sage*, but I was stuck.

Nothing clicked until I started scrolling through boy names and found *Kingsley*. The moment I saw it, it was like the universe whispered, *"This is you."* I wrote it down, ran upstairs to my mom, and told her. It wasn't just a name. It felt like the version of me I was meant to grow into.

At first, Kingsley was like a character, larger than life and fearless in ways I wasn't. On stage, she winked at the audience and owned every moment. But over time, I realized she wasn't just a persona. She was me, waiting for me to catch up.

The road to Kingsley wasn't always straightforward. For a while, I thought music education would be my path because it was practical. But one day, in a middle school band class, overwhelmed by the chaos, I realized: *This isn't it.*

I switched my major to vocal performance, leaving practicality behind for purpose.

Today, Kingsley isn't just a name: it's a mission. My work is about helping others step into their bold, authentic selves. My fanbase, *The Kingdom*, is a space where we celebrate unapologetic self-expression together. I wear many hats—artist, entrepreneur, creator—but at the heart of it all is the drive to connect, inspire, and make space for others to shine.

One of my favorite collaborations happened during the pandemic. I was walking one day and ran into Katherine from Event Cosmetics. I mentioned that I wasn't sure if I should release my album with everything going on. That's when she said, "Let's make lipsticks to go with your songs."

And we did. Together, we created lipsticks inspired by my music: *Therapy* (a matte black), *All Me* (a bold purple), and *I'm Fine* (a mood-changing gloss). Lipstick became another way to tell my story, to let people *wear* the emotions of my songs. Later, we added even more products, each tied to my music—a seamless blend of creativity and connection.

But Kingsley isn't just about music or lipsticks. It's about balance, fluidity, and honoring every part of the journey. My mornings are sacred—a time to ground myself with breathwork, gratitude, and reflection. It's my armor against the world's noise, a reminder that I'm in control of my narrative.

The biggest lesson I've learned is to trust my journey. My life coach, Dr. Esther, challenged me with an exercise: write my obituary. At first, it felt morbid, but it made me ask: *What do I want to leave behind?* The answer wasn't just music—it was authenticity. I want to create spaces where people feel safe to be their truest selves.

Looking back, I'm grateful for every twist and turn. My album, *Come and Find Me*, isn't just a collection of songs—it's a love letter to life, to messy, colorful, human moments. It's about finding beauty in the mundane and courage in vulnerability.

To my younger self, the girl who dared to dream of Kingsley: we did it. We became her. And to anyone chasing their own dream: hold it close, protect it, and share it with the world on your terms. When you're ready, celebrate it fully.

This is just the beginning. Every note, lyric, and beat is a piece of the world I'm building—one that reflects the stories I'm here to tell. Thank you for being part of it. Cheers to rainbows after the storm and every dream waiting to come to life.

We've only just begun.

This final piece I wrote is a letter to myself, and wow, this was emotional. I cried writing it and cried again reading it back. It's called *Welcome to the Kingdom*. The idea is that there's so much we don't know in the moment—things we only understand in hindsight. That's the theme that runs through my story: You didn't know it then, but look where you are now. So, I leave you with this…

## WELCOME TO THE KINGDOM: A LOVE LETTER TO KINGSLEY

To the little girl with big dreams and an even bigger voice…

Hey you, it's been a long time since we chatted…

You didn't know it then, but Kingsley saved you from yourself. Time and time again, she is the confidence you so desperately craved when you wanted to ask a boy to the dance but never did. She is the boldness you only had access to when anger was awry. She is the freedom you didn't know you deserved because you didn't always feel it.

You didn't know it then, but the only way the world made sense was when you became her.

You didn't know it then, but a name called to you. It is who you were truly meant to be. So, you ran to the computer and searched for her name. One that represented the star you knew you were meant to be. When you first heard it, it was like a scene from the movie *Chicago*. Now, you understand that you and Roxie shared the innocence of dreaming of a life of fame.

You didn't know it then, but the person you wished you could be was really you all along.

You didn't know then, that the first time you stepped on stage, a piece of home carved out in your heart would be there always and forever, no matter where you are in the world. A home that you can still come back to, even at 31 after spending two years traveling the world and you ended up being broker than ever, the stage would still be the only place that actually felt like home.

You didn't know it then, that on the opposite side of your depression was expression.

You didn't know it then, but the first song you wrote about the first boy you ever loved would be a revelation on how you process your emotions today. It is how you connect with the world around you, and it is how you use your voice to make others feel seen, heard, and loved.

You didn't know it then, but your third record, Come & Find Me, was a pivotal moment in finding yourself. Not just to be sexy but to feel it.

You didn't know it then, but finding your calling before you even knew who you were is a life not many get to have. Every moment when you haven't been on the right path still feels like it did in high school. When you went to state for the high jump and weren't the lead role in the musical. You sat in the music hallways away from your friends, and you cried so hard you thought you would never be able to cry again.

You didn't know it then, but you will break so many generational curses.

You didn't know it then, but your ability to captivate a crowd is a sacred gift. Though it started small in classrooms with friends and on talent show stages, you have and will always use it to create more joy, love, and happiness.

You didn't know it then, but you will become the Black girl you so desperately wished you saw in the media.

You didn't know it then, but your art would lead you to find your why in life. It would be the connector to all the strings in life that shed light on what brings you the most joy.

You didn't know it then, but your why is to help others become their most authentic selves.

You didn't know then, but your ability to chase after your dreams will inspire hundreds of others, so many that you lost track of names and locations of original connections. The way you boldly say what you want in life is so impactful others have no choice but to reach for higher.

You didn't know it then, but the world couldn't wait for you to arrive.

You didn't know it then, but you are a trailblazer. Someone who is willing to do whatever it takes to bring to life each and every idea you have—no matter the resources or how many no's you get—and you get a lot more nos than yeses. To courageously show the world each part of your becoming and magic in creations.

You didn't know it then, but you have always been my hero.

You didn't know then that I would even get the chance to write this letter to you with so much gratitude, grace, and love. Thank you for dreaming big enough to become Kingsley.

I love you xx,
Kingsley

# MY FAVORITE SONGS I'VE WRITTEN

Some of these songs are out on various streaming platforms,
if you want to listen.

## HIGHER

### (WRITTEN FOR THE AWAKEN THE TRAILBLAZER WITHIN PODCAST)

Paving my own ways.
Seeing light even in the darkest of days.
I trust myself and know my worth.
There is nothing but the stars behind me.

So can we go higher.
Can we go higher.

Together. We're better.
To dream bigger.

And louder.
Can we go higher.

So can we go higher
Can we go higher.

Together. We're better.
To dream bigger.
And louder.
Your aspirations are higher.

## BOW DOWN

Hi, my name is Kingsley
Yeah, I like to party
I've been drinking so much
Starting to get sleepy

Yeah, I'm newly single
But these boys are abysmal
I just want some head bro
I don't wanna beg though
Damn, this party's packed
Niggas don't know how to act
Wishing I was 21,

Maybe this shit would be fun

Ask me where my truth came from
I just found my way out
Moved into the me season
Yeah, I'm an Aries
I used to cry about men
Now I'm on my growth shit
I used to swear by this boy
Funny how that play out
All it took was time out
Making my own rules now
Oh, the crown fits better
When your hold your head up high

They said the queen is dead,
but the Kings here now

Take a look around everybody
Bow down, bow down

They said the queen is dead,
but the Kings here now, now, now

So bow down, down, down
So bow down, down, down


## ALL ME

Should of moved on
But you wanted to say

Should of let go
Had to go your own way
Now we're in this mess
Bitter as can better
Are you doing well
Are you doing well
Oh, without me, out me

I drank all my feelings
And I tried to stay sober
Fuck I can't lie, tried to move on
See, I'm right where you left me
And I drank up all my money
And I tried, I'm still lonely
Baby, don't lie, say you moved on
See, I'm right where you left me

Tell me is you
It is me
Say it's you
Cause it feels like it all me, all me

I drank all my feelings
I tried to stay sober
Fuck I can't lie, tired to move on
See, I'm right where you left me
I drank up all my money
I tried, I'm still lonely
Baby, don't lie and say you moved on
See, I'm right where you left me

Tell me is you
It is me
Say it's you
Cause it feels like it all me, all me

Should of known better
But I lost my head
Should of had it all

I chose pride instead
Now I'm all fucked up
Rotten to my core
See, I'm not doing well
I'm not doing well
Oh, when it's just me, just me

I drank all my feelings
And I tried to stay sober
Fuck I can't lie, tried to move on
See, I'm right where you left me

And I drank up all my money
And I tried, I'm still lonely
Baby, don't lie, say you moved on
See, I'm right where you left me

Tell me is you
It is me
Say it's you
Cause it feels like it all me, all me, all me


## BREAKING STILL

I'm still sad and you seem fine to me
I'm still mad, you'll never be right for me
How could I not be honest,
I believed your lies were promises
I'm, I'm still hurt, will I ever get over you

Tired of breaking my own damn heart
Oh, I'm tired of breaking my own heart
Oh, I'm tired of breaking still
Breaking, tired breaking still
Breaking still

I'm still sad looks like the worst part of me
I'm still mad but I don't wanna be
I let you take all of me,

Turned my love into a third degree
Oh, I'm still hurt, I'll never stop holding on,
I'm holding on

Tired of breaking my own damn heart
Oh, I'm tired of breaking my own heart
Oh, I'm tired of breaking still
Breaking, tired breaking still
Breaking still

Is there anybody out there
Tell me it'll be okay
Is there anybody out there
Who knows how to take the pain
So take it all, take it all away

Tired of breaking my own damn heart
Oh, I'm tired of breaking my own heart
Oh, I'm tired of breaking still
Breaking, tired breaking still
Breaking still


## LOVING YOU

What is this feeling, hole in my chest
I'm really dying, hardly get rest
I'm freaking out
How the hell are you so cool
Not gonna make it, gotta let go of you

Was I always this broken
Or did you wreck me
Was I always this fucked up
Or did you push me to be

Cause loving you
Worst thing I could do
Loving you, took all of me to lose
Loving you, loving you

What are we doing, I'm so confused
Two fucking years, no love I'm amused
See, I'm not okay
How the hell did you expect me to be
Hate to regret it
Need to let you go, I can't let you go, no

Was I always this broken
Or did you wreck me
Was I always this fucked up
Or did you push me to be

Cause loving you
Worst thing I could do
Loving you, took all of me to lose
Loving you, loving you x2

Looked past your damage, moved through the madness,
I am the beauty or the beast.
Lost in your habits, hearts couldn't be salvaged.
I loved you more than me

## STILL CRYING

Four years.
12 songs.
Waiting.
And here we are.
Long days.
Longer nights.
Hoping.
And here we are.

This what you truly wanted?
All this time, I ended up with nothing.
I held up longer than I should of, damn, you were my hardest lesson.

I don't wanna be still crying.
Still crying. Still crying. Still crying.

I don't wanna be still crying.
Still crying. Still crying. Still crying.

I prayed my love could make you change.
I loved you harder dispute the pain.
Can't believe I let it go on this way, I was fooled into thinking it is better for me to stay.
But someone had to walk away.
Put toxic love in its place.
I don't wanna be still crying.
Still crying. Still crying. Still crying.
I don't wanna be still crying.
Still crying. Still crying. Still crying.

No calls.
No texts.
Crying.
And here we are.

**SCAN TO MEET KINGSLEY**

# CHERYL HELLER

## SOBRIETY, STRENGTH & SWEETS

Early mornings are my favorite part of each day. In the quiet stillness, I reflect on my journey to this life I never thought I deserved. Every day, I am amazed at the miracles that allowed me to survive the darkest days and guided me into my new life.

I have been an alcoholic all my adult life. I started drinking to calm the crippling anxiety I've had as far back as I can remember. Throughout childhood, social situations often sent me spiraling into panic attacks. I was bullied in school, usually teased because my red hair and fair skin were different in our small town. I felt different from everyone else and never good enough. Mornings before school were filled with bleary-eyed piano practices; I was quizzed on spelling bee words during breakfast. Straight A's were the expectation, I would never have dared to bring home a B.

My younger sister was troubled and defiant from an early age, bringing constant upheaval to our home life. She was diagnosed with early onset schizophrenia at age 15; I learned in my mid-20s that she had endured familial sexual abuse from a very early age. Our home had no healthy coping mechanisms, so I sought comfort in food. I gained weight easily, prompting my mother to describe me as "thick in the middle."

I began throwing up regularly at age 7 and was an active bulimic for almost 40 years.

My drinking and bulimia intensified when I left home for college. I was depressed and homesick and gained a lot of weight my first year. Hiding my bulimia from my three roommates felt like a full-time job. I drank in my dorm room against university regulations. When I was caught, I grudgingly attended a required Alcohol 101 class that stressed the dangers of drinking. It made absolutely no impression on me.

One day, I passed out on my apartment's bathroom floor and woke to my roommate pounding on the door. I spent my nights drinking boxed wine and skipped classes most days. I failed one of my required senior year classes and almost didn't graduate. Someone in administration worked their magic, and I walked with my class. Looking back, I almost wish I would have had to deal then with the fallout of my bad choices. I wonder if it would have made a difference.

On the surface, my adult life seemed like a dream come true. After my divorce, my mother would often tell me, "But you had a perfect life. How could you possibly not have been happy?" No one understood the depth of my despair. I had a husband, two beautiful, healthy children, a good job, lots of friends, and a beautiful home, but I lived every day in a cesspool of misery.

I thought constantly of suicide and how my family's life would be better without me in it. I woke up every night with my heart pounding, blood rushing in my ears, unable to bring myself to say the word "alcoholic" but knowing it was true. And worrying that I would rot my teeth out of my head because of my bulimia. I agonized over secret credit card debt because I could not stop spending to fill the void of unhappiness. Terrified that I would be found out, that my secrets would be unearthed,

I could not stand the shame of it. Many nights, I snuck to the kitchen, filled my daughter's plastic cup with wine, and sat outside staring at the moon, quietly drinking as the demons faded and the edges of my depression blurred. I was drunk by the time the sun came up, both miserable and invigorated.

In 2013, I had been in the same job for seven years. The position was good for me, recruiting for a large bank. I started working in the office full-time, but after several years my teammates and I were allowed to work half days in the office and remotely as frequently as we liked. This was an ideal arrangement that allowed me to be home when my son got out of school and more flexibility, which helped with my anxiety.

I started grabbing a glass of wine when I got home from the office around 2 p.m. I poured the drinks a little earlier on the days I worked from home. This pattern continued for years, with no one the wiser. I often think back, how did they not see it? How did not one person realize what was going on? I was killing myself in front of everyone, and no one noticed.

This pattern continued for several years until my daughter turned five and entered kindergarten. I told my husband I wanted to change jobs because of my unhappiness with my new manager. This was true, but I also thought going back to an in-office position would help me curtail my day drinking. We hired an au pair, and I returned to work in the office.

The plan worked, in a way. I stopped drinking during the day but was completely miserable with the long commute and my new role, which was not as challenging as I'd hoped. I lasted about a year before quitting. The next job was a terrible fit for me. I was miserable from the first day.

I started going out at lunch, buying wine and drinking it in the parking lot. I did this to get through every agonizing minute of that job. I made it only a few months before changing jobs again. The new job was a better fit for me, but I was still unhappy overall and drinking heavily at night.

When I wasn't drinking, I was fantasizing about drinking. I had always been secretive about the amount I was consuming, and my husband, immersed in his own stressful job, did not seem to notice.

My alcoholism became public in early 2016. Our family had just returned from a Christmas vacation to Hawaii. I had supplemented our social drinking with the secret stash I'd packed in my suitcase. On my first day back at work, I planned to work remotely as our au pair had left for her own vacation. My husband was getting ready to leave for work and caught me sneaking wine at 7 a.m.

It is difficult to adequately describe the pain of that time. The next several years were a nightmarish blur. I agreed to seek treatment and started attending an evening outpatient group that met each night after work. This was my first experience of spending time with other alcoholics and addicts, and I found it incredibly draining. The meetings did nothing to help, instead intensifying my depression and unhappiness. I continued drinking and started coming to my meetings under the influence. I ended up getting kicked out of the group for showing up drunk.

I so desperately wanted an end to my unhappiness, and I admitted myself into an out-of-state rehab facility. The experience was completely foreign to me. Not drinking was difficult, but surprisingly, almost immediately, I sank into the opportunity to rest my body and mind.

The overall experience was positive, and I did have some hope, but faced with the reality of returning to my unhappy home life, I drank on the plane coming home. I continued secretly drinking every morning before work and spent unhappy evenings waiting until everyone went to bed so I could drink alone. I left my office around noon one day during that time and headed to a restaurant where I had a few drinks at the bar.

I bought a bottle of wine at the liquor store next door and drove home. When I got there, I used the bottle of wine to wash down a bottle of sleeping pills. Laying in my guest room, I panicked when I realized my kids might find me when they got home from school. I called my husband and told him what I had done.

He took me to the hospital, where I spent several days in the psychiatric unit. I was released, came home, returned to work, and repeated the cycle. Over the next two years, I went to rehab multiple times, had several suicide attempts, and was repeatedly kicked out of our home for being drunk.

I spent a few months in and out of extended-stay suites, unable to comprehend what I was doing to myself and my family. My addiction had become the single driving force of my life. I knew I couldn't continue to live this way, almost homeless, no longer a mother or wife. I asked my husband for a divorce and moved into an apartment.

Without anyone to monitor my drinking, I plummeted further into a hellish existence. I began drinking from the time I woke up until I staggered to bed each night. I signed divorce papers that minimized my parental rights and left me with almost nothing. My very existence relied upon alcohol. It completely consumed me. Every waking thought was about getting the next drink. Any semblance of normalcy was long gone. Work, family, friends, everything had washed away in a sea of alcohol.

My divorce was finalized in April of 2017. I moved from the apartment to a small house outside of our community. I was not able to see my children, and I needed geographical distance from my ex-husband and the shame of my public humiliation. That August, my rental house flooded during a hurricane. I moved into a hotel while my house was being repaired and met my current husband while staying there.

Our early relationship was anything but smooth. Together, we navigated the fallouts of devastating divorces and my worsening alcohol addiction. I could not and did not want to stop drinking. I had a glimpse of happiness with my new relationship but was so far into my addiction that it was a part of me, as much as my arms and legs. My new love agonized over my drinking, but he did not police me.

The next years were a continuation of pain and self-abuse. My dad died suddenly in July 2018, leaving our family shell-shocked. I numbed myself with alcohol, I got fired from yet another job, my face and body puffy as I continued to down the alcohol that was insidiously destroying me from the inside out. From that job, I moved to another that was fine enough, but my addiction required me to drink constantly throughout the day to avoid tremors.

Each morning, I tucked my water bottle filled with vodka into my work backpack and set off on the bus. Every day, all day, I drank vodka mixed with Coke Zero. I continued down this path for about 8 months until early 2020 when I started getting sick at work every day.

I felt fine each morning but was seized by a crippling fatigue every day around noon. I regularly took an Uber home, laying in the back seat, softly crying from pain and exhaustion. During this time, whispers of what would become the COVID pandemic were stirring. That's what is wrong with me, I thought; I have COVID.

In early March, we booked a murder mystery weekend at a bed and breakfast. I was so sick that I missed the entire event. I spent the entire time upstairs, the door cracked, listening to laughter from downstairs as I threw up hundreds of times in the vintage bathroom. Each time I recovered from a vomiting episode, I mixed another drink. I spent the entire weekend drinking and throwing up. This was not bulimia, which had evaporated in the background as if it had never been, an unrealized miracle eclipsed by my drinking. This was, I learned later, early-stage liver failure. After that weekend, we received word that our office was closing due to the pandemic, and we would be working remotely.

I watched the horror of the pandemic unfold as I isolated myself and drank. I also continued throwing up multiple times a day. I was seized by violent nausea and threw up bile or just dry heaved, lying by the toilet shaking and sweating. This cycle of constant drinking and vomiting continued for several months.

I woke up on June 30, 2020, and looked in the mirror. To my horror, my skin and the whites of my eyes had turned yellow overnight. I didn't know what to do, so I tried to cover my yellow skin with makeup and started to work. I was drinking, as usual, and joined a video conference with several of my team members. I don't know exactly why, but the next morning, I was released from my contract position.

My husband took me to the emergency room, where I was diagnosed with cirrhosis and hospitalized. I spent two weeks in the hospital, with no visitors because of COVID, receiving fluids and stern warnings from the doctors and hospital staff. When I finally recovered enough to be released, the first thing I did was pour a glass of wine. I drank two large bottles of chardonnay that day, getting so drunk that I could not even stand up from the couch without falling. I could not stop drinking, even though I now had confirmation that I was dying.

My new gastroenterologist recommended a procedure to check for esophageal fissures, common in alcoholics and potentially fatal. When I woke up from the procedure, my doctor and boyfriend were standing at my bedside. My doctor said that by some miracle I did not have notable esophageal damage. He also told me that if I did not quit drinking, I would be dead within a couple of months. He asked me if I might give not drinking one more try. I stared at him.

How could I stop?

I had proven to myself that I was willing to destroy my life, to purposely kill myself. I could not imagine my life without the soft cocoon of alcohol warming my body, keeping me alive, and giving me the strength to get through one more day. But those were not the words that came out of my mouth. Instead, I told him, I will try. I do not think I can do it, but I will try. He sent me home with some pills to stop my withdrawal tremors, and I made an appointment to meet with his team the next week.

I spent those first sober days on my couch, listening to my husband work in the next room as I drank bottles of non-alcoholic champagne and watched hours of television. I watched as my swollen yellow feet leaked fluid from old surgical scars onto the floor.

My doctors told me to prepare for the worst.

I met with a liver transplant specialist who told me I would not qualify to be on the transplant list until I had been sober for six months.

She didn't know if I would make it that long.

I prepared my will and power of attorney. I filled up like a water balloon and endured multiple surgeries to drain excess fluids from my body. In the shower, I stared at my belly, swollen like a full-term pregnancy.

I cried, and I prayed.

I drank bottles of non-alcoholic champagne and hundreds of bottles of nutrient-rich mineral water. I took diuretics and vitamins, made weekly trips to the hospital for surgeries, cried more, and began to reflect on my situation. My swelling gradually reduced, and my skin tone returned to normal.

My physical appearance at 60 days sober was astounding. I looked almost healthy. My doctors were surprised and encouraged. For the first time in what seemed like forever, I had hope. I think of myself as a baby bird in those early days, so weak that I could barely move, terrified to leap back into the world.

By October, I felt strong enough to return to work. I found a new job in an office, a rarity in COVID times. I commuted to work daily, drank bottles of mineral water, ate healthy foods, engaged with my co-workers, and returned home each day exhausted but almost happy.

I started to see a light.

My body was continuing to respond to treatment. Talk of a liver transplant faded as my liver enzyme levels continued to drop. I embraced the principles of Alcoholics Anonymous for the first time. I started an alcohol monitoring program where I blew into a breathalyzer three times a day, a practice I continued for almost three years. I started a new job, the one I have now, which allows me to work remotely full-time. I enrolled in a debt reduction plan and am about to graduate four years later.

That first year, I walked over 1500 miles, sobbing and praying with each step as I shed my addiction from my mind, body, and soul. After a year of sobriety, I hired a new attorney and armed with the data from my monitoring program, was granted partial custody of my daughter.

On my one-year sober anniversary, I shared my story at an alumni meeting at one of the rehab facilities I had attended. After the meeting, two women with yellowed, jaundiced eyes and skin approached me and told me my story had given them hope.

I speak at an AA meeting on my sober birthday each year, essential service work to help other alcoholics who are still suffering. My husband and I eloped in October 2022, two years after I almost died. He quit drinking with me in solidarity on July 22, 2020, when I was reborn as a person with hope. I have embraced my new life with a joy I didn't know was possible.

I turned 50 in 2023 and dedicated most of the year to my personal transformation. I engaged a life coach and began practicing transcendental meditation. Through these experiences. I have learned how to practice healthy self-care and gained the ability to love myself. I also started a cottage bakery business, a true passion project and, I think, a miracle for a former bulimic.

My life today is one I could never have imagined. Over the past four years, I have learned to use healthy coping skills. I am kind to myself. I set boundaries and keep them. I face my fears and challenges head-on rather, no longer burying them in alcohol and other destructive behaviors.

My cirrhosis is stable, more a chronic condition than a worry. I have partial custody of my daughter, and soon, she will begin living with me full-time during the school year.

I have a strong relationship with my son and daughter. I'm in a happy, healthy marriage. I am my sister's guardian. I find inner peace in meditation and swim 4–5 miles every week. I have a rewarding full-time job and a thriving small business. I have loyal friends who understand my journey and forgive me for my past actions.

I now understand God's will for me and how to fulfill it in this life. My days are filled with family, service work, and being the best version of myself. I have many battle scars, and I wear them with pride. I will never forget how far I have come. I am a survivor.

SCAN TO MEET CHERYL

# AYESHA SODHA

## RISE, ROAR & REINVENT

I sat across the table from my fiancé in disbelief as he explained: "It's not that I don't want to marry you. It's that I don't want to sponsor your visa. When will you get your six-figure salary?"

We had already spent the last three months apart while I worked in London, and just a week before, he'd wavered for days about whether he really wanted to get married. Then, he explained to me that he'd gotten cold feet but apparently had gotten over them. He continued, "Maybe you don't have enough education behind you to really succeed here. Maybe you should go back to law."

I thought to myself, *The salary doesn't come because the visa sponsorship limits my offers.* Let's not forget that in the time it took him to get his one six-figure job offer, I'd landed three offers. And he had just finished his MBA and was 10 years older than me. I already had a flight booked to go back to London the next day, which I fully intended to cancel, as my lawyer had advised we simply sign the paperwork and apply for the visa before I left the country. We had even spoken to our priest the day before about wedding date options. Yet, there I was, staring in disbelief. My final line: "If you don't trust me enough to sponsor my visa, you certainly shouldn't be marrying me."

That night, I packed my bags, sipping vodka and crying. Four years in New York packed into three suitcases. My job had ended two weeks earlier, and now, so had my relationship. I called my uncle and asked him to pick me up from the airport, no questions asked. I felt a wave of relief when he agreed.

On the plane from New York back to the UK—the place I swore I could never live again—I cried the entire time. What the hell had just happened to my life?

The next two weeks were a blur. I slept all day and stayed up all night. I avoided anything that reminded me of New York. Failure echoed in my mind. I had no job, no home, and my fiancé—the second most important man in my life—had rejected me, just as my father had. I had shamed my family, after a massive engagement ceremony with 150 relatives eight months earlier. How would my family announce this? How could I tell people that my relationship failed because I wasn't a good financial investment?

After two weeks of crying, my mother called me. "I don't care what's going on," she said, "I want you home with me." So, I packed up again and returned to Edinburgh—the last place on earth I wanted to be. I had despised it when I lived there before. But I had no direction, no plan, no choices. I moved into my mother's box room, using an old phone and a limited wardrobe. My fabulous New York couture had no place on Edinburgh's cold cobbled streets. Over the next few months, I continued to sleep all day and stay awake at night. I imagined driving my car off Waverley Bridge. That would take away the shame, right? Still, there were moments when I fantasized about him coming to the UK, apologizing, and begging me to come back.

My mother owns a health and wellness company, which turned out to be my saving grace. She got the flu and needed someone to cover for her, so I filled in for two weeks. My ex would call periodically, suggesting I find a job that would sponsor me, so we'd have more time to decide. When I told him it was time to move on, he laughed. "Move on? You're just waiting for me. Helping out in your mother's shop doesn't count as a career." It didn't help that my mother kept making excuses for his behavior.

Then the email came. He wanted to split the cost of sending my belongings back, even though he had kept all the money from our engagement, and my family had paid for the party in full. My ego refused to take anything of monetary value. His family's gifts? I left them behind. His mother, who had been so eager for us to marry, now thought it wasn't a good idea—likely because they'd seen my family's wealth and found it lacking. When my mother read that email, she finally understood. "It's like hearing your father all over again," she said.

And that's when it hit me: There was no respect, no love. History had repeated itself. I wasn't good enough for them—just as I hadn't been good enough for my father. I remembered something I'd read about the universe giving you knocks, harder and harder, until you learn your lesson.

That didn't dull the pain. I hadn't driven my car off the bridge, though. The thought of what it would do to my mother stopped me. So, I had two choices: life or death. I made myself a bucket list of things I'd regret not doing if my life ended tomorrow. All the hunger inside me ignited again.

I was going to live. Misery was never my favorite color, anyway. But where to start? I was broken, with no confidence, no career path, and no idea what to do next. I'll take you back to my mother's well-being center. Most of her staff knew me and decided they would find a way to heal me. Having an emotional, physical, and mental collapse meant that all new healing therapies could be trialed on me first. Each therapist gave me a nugget, some multiple sessions. I realized that with my history repeating itself—with men in my life telling me I wasn't good enough—there was a pattern. And if I didn't find a way to break it, things would get much worse.

I had theta healing. I did a full weekend of healing, focused on being connected to a higher source and washing away trauma without spending 20 years in therapy. I did shaking therapy, introduced to trauma victims in Africa. I had German new medicine sessions with kinesiology. I read. I journaled. I cried and cried, and then cried some more. I was completely unhinged at times. I broke further, but somehow I knew it was part of the process.

The big one was self-realization. There had been a pattern in my recent relationships of being made to feel like I was financially incapable, unstable, and useless. Of course, people come into your life as mirrors. This had zero to do with them and everything to do with me. I was feeling financially insecure and incompetent. I had no investments, no great salary, never had. And moreover, I knew nothing about money. I knew I wanted to make it, but I was clueless. So, what would make me feel financially secure? I decided: a property. Bricks and mortar of my own. This became my goal. And I decided I wouldn't get into any relationships until I had hit this goal.

Distractions were in abundance. My aunt even put me on every dating website the moment I arrived back in the country. She said it was good for my confidence. One of the most notable experiences I had was a Tarot card reading. The reader sat me down and said, "This is a whole new movie. One where you're writing the script, producing, directing, acting in, and designing." It didn't hit me until later, but that became my biggest lesson in life.

From the rollercoaster of healing, one day, I was in a German new medicine session when it struck me that parents do the best they can with what they know. If they weren't the parent you wanted or used a style you didn't prefer, it's not personal. Their behavior is learned from their experiences.

Boom! It was like I had spent my life breathing with one lung, and now I had two. I was flying after that. Maybe it was all the work I had done, but it was worth it. I felt like a phoenix rising from the ashes.

A friend who was similarly lost in life—feeling financially reliant on his partner and unfulfilled—suggested we meet for coffee and figure out our lives. It was a life strategy brainstorm. My control-freak self had to put structure around it, so we grabbed paper, colored pens, and Post-its. We wrote down a bunch of questions to brainstorm and swapped notes. Within six months, our lives were unrecognizable, and we were on the path to everything we wanted.

I had just returned from a business trip to China and India, working on two incredible projects that I loved. I was exhausted, but I was flying high. I was supposed to spend a few days with my then-boyfriend, a man I couldn't decide was right or wrong for me. We had spent months fighting on and off. He was the best I had ever dated—he worshiped me, loved my fire, and appreciated my Leo nature, something I had been conditioned to apologize for. He was a genius, and within our first month, he had told me I was the woman he wanted to marry.

I arrived, and he was late. I ordered a glass of wine to calm my nerves. I just couldn't figure it out. He was amazing, but he never had money, couldn't commit to plans, and let me down repeatedly. He borrowed money from my family behind my back and would make plans, then flake, over and over. He once showed up for a group holiday booking with just 12 hours' notice. What was the deal? Was he right for me or not?

That day we simply talked, drank, and somehow got on the same page. At his house later, he insisted we sleep in the bed on his mezzanine floor, which I had already fallen from on a previous trip. There was no rail, no light. That night, I got up to go to the bathroom and literally walked off the mezzanine, falling three meters and hitting a table on my way down. The paramedics were called, and I was taken to the hospital.

As I lay there in shock, they ran emergency scans. Initially, they found no major damage. I was relieved, thinking I could still make my upcoming project in India in three months. But soon after, they discovered I had fractured my hip. I was moved from room to room as they treated me. I still remember watching the needle as they stitched my lip back together.

The next morning, coming off morphine, they explained the full extent of my injuries: severe bone bruising in both knees, a fractured hip, a chipped tooth, bruises all over my face, herniated discs, and I had lost part of my lower lip. The radiologist explained that once my hip healed, they would need to operate on the herniated discs to prevent paralysis. I sat in my hospital bed, alone, and wept. What the actual fuck just happened? My work was amazing. I was doing what I loved. Was I about to lose my entire life?

My boyfriend arrived and told me he had begged the doctors to fix my face because I was public-facing in my job. He said, "Thank God, you're okay. I had already decided last night that if anything happened to you, you would be my responsibility for life." A noble gesture, I thought. He took incredible care of me over the next two weeks, cutting my food into tiny pieces, wheeling me around the hospital, and showering me instead of the nurse because I felt safer with him. He helped in ways my mother couldn't, though she was shocked at how bad things were when she arrived.

The reality was that I had almost died—saved by a hair's breadth. One millimeter in the wrong direction, and the outcome would have been catastrophic. So, I said thank you to the universe and asked again, *What do I need to learn from this?*

I dedicated myself to recovery, staying as positive as I could. They told me if I hindered my hip's regrowth, I'd need a replacement, so I followed every instruction carefully. When it was time to return to my own place, my boyfriend was supposed to meet me in London and help me transition back to normal life. But he never showed. Fortunately, my amazing friends stepped in to help. But the man I had thought might be the one? Nowhere to be found.

I didn't end up needing the spinal surgery. The UK deemed it unnecessary, and while they never reviewed my scans properly, I took it as a sign that my body was healing itself. My London physio told me I'd never pole dance again, a passion I had pursued seriously before the accident. I thought, *Fuck that, watch me.* I threw myself into strengthening my body. Eleven months later, I was stronger than ever, and I celebrated with a photoshoot to capture my progress. You never know when things could change.

After five months of physio, I was learning to walk again. I still remember the day I stepped onto the beach and felt the sand under my feet. I vowed never to take walking for granted again. From that moment, my healing accelerated. Nature is important.

My learnings?

There is no guarantee of tomorrow, so enjoy what you have. Goals are important but capture your journey. I realized I had been waiting to celebrate until I reached a certain point, but life is about the steps along the way. If you don't learn your lessons early enough, the universe will land you on your ass until you make a change.

The world was going nuts over COVID, but it felt distant, like a "Chinese thing." I had just returned from a business trip with my Australian boss—a road trip we had planned for months. Towards the end of the trip, travel restrictions tightened, but I still managed to take a key in-person meeting. COVID hit the UK, but I felt untouched.

Back home, lockdown began, and I was excited—twelve weeks in one place! I created a Pinterest board of all the projects I would tackle. A friend reminded me that while everyone was talking about how to avoid COVID, no one was preparing for what to do if you caught it. I stocked up on essentials, just in case.

On day one of lockdown, I got one symptom, then a second. I immediately isolated. It wasn't too bad; I just worked through it. After the quarantine period ended, I thought I was better—until I crashed. I couldn't get out of bed and dragged myself through the days. Weeks passed, and the symptoms worsened—chest tightness, headaches, and an inability to focus. The NHS told me to call an ambulance if I thought I was dying, but I didn't want to die in a hospital. For eight weeks, it felt like an elephant was sitting on my chest.

My friends fell away, treating me like a leper. The life I had celebrated—financial independence, travel, freedom—now felt like a death sentence. I imagined dying alone in my flat, eaten by Scottish rats.

Finally, a doctor saw me in week fourteen. All my vitals were normal, but I could barely walk down the street. She seemed excited to study me as a long COVID case.

A friend's cousin recommended rest, something I hadn't tried yet. I flew to Spain to recover with my mum. My company gave me four weeks of paid sick leave. I couldn't walk, pick up a mug, or even scramble an egg without pain. But I looked "normal," and people assumed I was making it up.

Then, after months of relapses, I started to feel better. Slowly, the relapses became less frequent, and I returned to work.

One day, while video-chatting with my tenant back in Edinburgh, she said something strange. "I wasn't sure whether to tell you, but when I moved the bed to access the pole for exercise, I found something under it. I showed it to my mentor, and they confirmed it was a voodoo curse. Just be careful about who you let into your home."

Shocked, I asked her when she had found it. "About ten days ago," she replied. I paused, and it suddenly hit me that my health had dramatically improved around the same time. My mother and I immediately thought of the same person who could have placed the curse. It made me think deeply about the energy and people I allowed into my life.

After this unsettling discovery, I decided to move forward. I was even more determined to live life fully and embrace the changes.

I realized COVID had been the push I needed to leave Scotland, and I started planning a new chapter in London. But life had other plans. I booked a ten-day trip to Dubai to visit a friend. While there, new COVID strains hit the UK, and flights were canceled. Dubai introduced remote-working visas, allowing residents to get vaccinated immediately, so I decided to stay.

Within weeks, I started considering Dubai my home. I attended intellectual discussions, explored investment opportunities, and eventually started my own consultancy. I embraced the change, realizing that life had a way of delivering what you needed, even if the path was unexpected.

My learnings?

You never know how long your life—or your body's capabilities—will last. Take risks. It's just money; what doesn't come back is your time. Do what makes you happy. Life is too short for anything else. Be mindful of the energy and people you let into your life. The universe always has your back. What you ask for may come in ways you didn't expect, but it will always be what you need.

SCAN TO MEET AYESHA

# BÉATRICE RECOUSSINE

## CANCER, FAMILY & BEING PRESENT

People tell me my story inspires them. I don't know if it's what happened in my life or how I survived. I was born and raised in France. I had a happy childhood with my parents, my brother, and my sister. Love and respect were the strongest values of my family.

When I met my husband, I told him if he needed to move abroad for his job, I would follow him. My dad worked abroad for most of his career. He was often absent, and I missed him a lot. I didn't want to be separated from someone I loved again. The first opportunity for my husband arose in 2005. We moved with two daughters from Bordeaux, France, to Casablanca, Morocco.

Expatriation is an exciting adventure, but it can also be complex and stressful. I needed to reinvent my life and adapt to a new culture, develop new intercultural skills, and cope with being away from my homeland.

How would I manage life out of my comfort zone?

Even though it's possible to speak French in Casablanca, I learned basic Arabic words to communicate. At this time, I was busy developing my business as a life coach. I was always in action, and I didn't really understand the need to slow down. After six amazing years in Casablanca, where we welcomed the birth of our son, and I worked hard on my business, my husband had another opportunity.

In 2011, we arrived in Dallas, Texas, USA. My priority was to help my family transition. A few months later, I was hired as the executive director of Alliance Française de Dallas to promote French culture. In my spare time, I studied English. I had learned some English in middle school, but I was not able to speak English when I arrived in Dallas. As director, I needed to make speeches, and it was very stressful. I was out of my comfort zone speaking English, especially in front of an audience.

However, I learned a lot. I enjoyed managing my team and setting up projects in Dallas. Gradually, I improved my second language, even though I kept my French accent! I had a happy life I only dreamed of living that included a loving husband with three beautiful children. We traveled a lot to discover this new country. We loved our adventures! The last family trip was to Arizona, with its incredible canyons. My favorite was Antelope Canyon with beams of light and a magical spirit.

In 2017, my life turned upside down. My sweet nine-year-old son was diagnosed with brain cancer. I resigned from the job I loved to focus on him and started down a long road. I didn't realize my new job was a caregiver. Because I was the mom, it was a given I would be with him. I was his caregiver, and this role would be the hardest job I ever had! I needed to leave my team, and I was so grateful another employee took the lead for the organization.

Living in this tsunami, far from my family in France and speaking a second language, was very scary and challenging. I didn't know all the medical words in English, and my son decided to express his anger only in French. To be honest, I did not translate to the medical team all the emotions coming out of my son's mouth! I didn't know he knew so many colorful words, especially at nine years old!

I learned the hard way that it's normal to feel afraid, angry, sad, and overwhelmed (sometimes, all in one day).

I wouldn't have survived without the love of my husband and daughters, and all the support we received from family, friends, and communities. Cancer is a family disease, and I wasn't the only one traumatized. My husband was a trooper during this adversity. We were very proud of our daughters, who faced the calamity with strength. The link between us became so much stronger. I have tears in my eyes thinking of how this affected their lives as well.

I lost my desire to eat or cook. A friend created a train meal for us, and we received food for many days. It was so generous, and we received so much love and support! I didn't know kindness helped me develop a new skill: Resilience and Never Give Up was my mantra! I tried to make every day a beautiful day!

We started on the Intensive Care journey. My first memory was a night we were with the neurosurgeon, in a little room, with MRI images of the cancer in our son's brain in front of us. Time stood still. I asked if my son could survive. He answered yes, but he needed to set up the surgery immediately. I left the room and took off my scarf because I couldn't breathe. My husband, who was terrorized, found the strength to hug me. We cried together.

On October 20, 2017, at 11:15 a.m., we arrived at emergency. We met with the neurosurgeon at 1 p.m., and he informed us there was a mass on our son's brain. The MRI was planned for 5 p.m. Technicians came and hugged me after the MRI was done, which was unusual because the technicians usually didn't give us any hugs... Something was wrong for sure! We met the neurosurgeon again at 10 p.m. again with MRI images, and the surgery started at 7 a.m. on October 21. The surgery seemed like an eternity, more than six hours. The only thing you would see in our eyes was fear: the fear of losing our beautiful boy.

After the surgery, it took three weeks to recover, and the remaining tumors grew very fast. Because of this new emergency, the hospital opened the radiotherapy unit, over the weekend, so they could begin radiation treatment immediately to prevent him from becoming paralyzed for the rest of his life. Despite the fear, we were grateful they did this for him and for us. Our son had radiation for six weeks, five days per week. We were fortunate the center of proton therapy was only twenty minutes from home. Then came the chemo for six months. He lost his hair, but the biggest shock was he had no eyebrows. He was so very pale and skinny. We knew it was the only solution to treat the cancer, but it was heartbreaking to watch him decline.

My son told me one day, "Mom, cancer doesn't like love and laughter." I said, "You have so much love around you, we need to figure out how to get some laughter into the hospital."

So, we began creating memories that would make us laugh.

One day, I went to Walmart to find inspiration in red, my son's favorite color. There was only one red costume. I bought it and went to visit my son, as a lobster. Many people smiled at me; however, my only goal was to see a smile on the beautiful face of my son.

My son's friends came to visit him at the hospital and played with the plastic gloves. They looked like chickens to them. They were laughing with my son, and it was wonderful hearing their laughter. They don't know how much they touched my heart that day.

My best friend, who came to visit from France, had a crazy laugh. Every time we sat on the sofa, there was a malfunction, and the sofa opened. Our laughter still rings in my ears.

My son was playing with his sister in the waiting room before his treatment. They played with their hair, and my son didn't have hair anymore, because of chemo. He played with his imagination. We had a crazy laugh, and it was contagious because other people started smiling with us. It's a place of heavy vibes usually.

We found laughter and joy on our dark, scary journey.

I realized we needed to take better care of ourselves. The road was long, and I was exhausted. A nurse sat beside me and gave me permission to take care of myself during this journey. I returned to my Pilates classes, I was not a selfish person who abandoned a sick son, but I needed to refill my energy tank. Pilates helped me do that.

Meditation and conscious breathing were also my allies in adversity.

We can't feel guilty if we take five minutes for ourselves. Guilt is a common feeling of caregivers, but it's vital to find a way to be re-energized!

The BIG thing I've overcome is that now I live each moment more intensely. I savor my life. My son is a survivor, and I could not be more grateful! Helping others enjoy their lives is my new purpose! We don't need to stay in a sad place: We deserve to be happier.

I love the French book, *Consolation* by Anne Dauphine Julliand. She explains that when we suffer, we need others more than ever, and hugs are extremely important during those moments! I agree with her, we need hugs. We don't need advice, which is often judgmental, but rather we need support.

October 2019: My son had something that resembled a stroke. Doctors told us it was a virus, and our son was in remission. We felt relieved like we were walking on a cloud. May 2020: He had a second one, and our son was not able to speak anymore.

In December 2020, I faced a new challenge. My dad was diagnosed with cancer. He passed away on March 3, 2021. His cancer was very aggressive. I collapsed, it was too much for me, losing my dad without being able to visit him during the summer of the pandemic.

On top of that, not being able to communicate with my son was another new challenge. I felt as if I was never going to overcome this sadness, I was done. Why did all of this happen to my family? Why would it never stop? Why couldn't we see the light at the end of this dark tunnel?

I took antidepressants to survive.

I didn't want anymore.

I was so tired of fighting.

Love from family and friends helped.

My son helped me with his resilience: after many sessions of speech therapy, he could speak again.

I had tears when he could again tell me, "I love you, Mom." In 2023, after merely surviving for several years, I decided to align my life with what makes me tick. I left a job that never fulfilled me but had good health insurance.

I set up my business as a health and life coach to help people when their lives are filled with unexpected trauma. I began coach training and received a new certification. And I transformed my habits of sadness into habits of happiness.

Two quotes continue to help me a lot:

"You may not control all the events that happen to you, but you can decide not to be reduced by them." —Maya Angelou

"Happiness is not the absence of problems; it's the ability to deal with them."
—My mother-in-law

## LIFE LESSONS LEARNED:

- Yes, it's possible to change your perception of a situation. I started feeling better when I chose to see the positive instead of the negative.

- I realized how much gratitude can help you; there is always something to feel grateful for.

- Good health is the best thing we can hope for!

- I need to nourish and cherish my body by exercising every day and eating the healthiest foods possible. Because my body deserves to be treated kindly and needs to be loved.

- Sometimes, you need to end some relationships for your mental health and maintain relationships with people who really help you.

- Living in the present moment is powerful to feel more joy in life.

Spending endless days in the hospital, I realized there is little emotional support there for parents going through this scary journey. So, I am volunteering at a hospital for pediatric cancer support groups to help parents, and at Hopekids to help moms on this frightening, lonely road. I hope the medical system can see and hear how necessary these groups are for parents. We can't leave them all alone. I hope that the medical system can offer this type of support in the future, a place where the parents can safely share their emotions.

Life is full of challenges and obstacles that can leave us overwhelmed and fearful. Whether it's a traumatic event from our past or a current situation causing us distress, it's important to remember we have the power to overcome our fears and live a happier, more fulfilling life.

Today, I know that living in a dark place can destroy you.

Today, I am savoring my life and enjoying more of it each moment. I choose activities that give me energy and I meditate, as well. Walking in nature daily is fascinating; I can pay more attention to what happens around me. I see different animals. A few days ago, I met two coyotes on the road... these animals were fascinating, and I wasn't afraid. I believe they gave me strong energy that day.

To boost and challenge myself, I am trying a new activity each month. For example, I am making patisserie or trying recipes my family enjoys. I am also doing yoga now.

And guess what? I am no longer afraid to try something new! I am enjoying it!

There are angels around us. Our family had many angels who held our hands and walked with us on this cancer journey. I thank them every day from the bottom of my heart.

This year, we are celebrating, with a big party, the milestone of five years cancer-free for my son. My family still thinks about those kids in the hospital now, and especially those who will be there during the holidays. We suggested the guests bring gifts for them. We received one hundred toys, and it was an honor to deliver them to the hospital. My son accompanied us to his old 6th floor. I wanted to hug all the parents and bring them hope because I've been in their place.

My family enjoys playing cards and games together. These important moments are so precious for us. Spending time together and enjoying these little things are now the most important thing. We continue to have fun and laugh. Jokes are so very welcome in my family! I believe we all forget how important it is. Life is not about being serious. Life is continuing to play and express our inner child!

Before everything happened, I wouldn't have been able to change family plans for my work, but today I put my family in first place! And I am enjoying every hug I receive. I don't need material gifts: I appreciate spending time with the ones I love. When my children ask me what I want for Mother's Day, my answer is simple: I want a moment with you. This is most important for me, having each precious moment with my children in good health.

Do I regret my decision to return to my career coaching? It was the best decision of my life! I feel so nourished to help people to feel better in their lives. I am happy to see their smiles. I am happy when they share their successes with me. I am still impressed to see how much potential each of us has! One of my clients shared that before meeting me, she had suicidal thoughts. Now, seeing her enjoy her life fully is a gift for me.

Most of my decisions today are made with my heart.

If my story resonates with you and if you want to improve your life, I would love to hear from you and would be honored to support you in your transformation. I hope you've found some inspiration here with my story.

SCAN TO MEET BÉATRICE

# ABBIE WESTGATE

## BURNOUT, BREATHWORK & POLICE WELLNESS

Joining the police in 2018 was a dream come true, and putting on my uniform for the first time was a 'pinch me' moment, one I'd envisioned many times growing up. But when that acceptance letter finally arrived through the door, it was bittersweet. Instead of celebrating, I was planning my mum's funeral, struggling to comprehend how such a special achievement had become tainted with so much sadness.

Starting a career in the police is challenging at any stage of life, one that nothing can truly prepare you for, but navigating that journey from the depths of grief made me feel so isolated and alone. To my new colleagues, I was a stranger, and my grief went unseen, so I buried it quietly and dedicated myself to a life of service.

Although I pushed the grief and trauma deep down, it was silently wreaking chaos beneath the surface. Within a few months, I reached the end of a six-year relationship with my fiancé, and the life I once knew slipped even further from my grasp.

Having always been praised for my 'strength and resilience' and my ability to 'push forward in the face of adversity', I did what I knew best. I stayed busy, pushed things out of my mind, hit the gym, and worked hard. This mindset was reinforced further by my promotion to sergeant within three years, which gave me a sense of control in the chaos, and still remains one of the proudest moments of my life!

Then in 2022, a collision of events in my personal and professional life caused everything to come crashing down. I experienced heightened and prolonged levels of stress and anxiety, eventually leading to severe burnout. With nowhere to hide, the unprocessed trauma lying dormant surfaced, and my physical health suffered. Things got so bad I once rang for an ambulance, convinced I was having a heart attack.

A real highlight of my policing career was being awarded a Certificate of Commendation from the Royal Humane Society, for assisting in saving the life of a woman, and yet I didn't even know how to save myself—the irony wasn't lost on me!

In the 'masculine' world of policing, there was little room for vulnerability, and the fear of losing the only thing I had left, my career—stopped me from seeking the help I desperately needed, leaving my spirit broken. At my lowest point, I was suicidal and planning to end my own life. Thankfully my story didn't end there, but it was clear the way I'd been running my mind, body, and life desperately needed to change.

The turning point came when I sat down to write a goodbye letter, intending to leave some beautiful, comforting words to ease my family's pain but found nothing to say; surely my life was worth more than a blank sheet of paper?

I knew I couldn't leave that way! I looked down at the notebook and began ripping at the pages before throwing it off the wall. I made a promise to myself—if I was staying on this earth, I had to find a way to heal. I didn't know what this looked like, or if it was even possible, but I would spend the rest of my life trying.

This wholehearted commitment seemed to unlock a door within my life, and a new path appeared—I followed blindly, not knowing where it would lead. Little did I know, I'd just taken the first step on a profound healing journey that would change my entire life path.

Aware my stress levels were dangerously high and terrified of experiencing another 'heart attack', I began meditating, which is how I accidentally found myself in a breathwork class one day (or did breathwork find me?!).

In that session, I finally let go of emotions buried deep: grief, betrayal, hurt, sorrow, anger, frustration... All moved through me like someone had just released a pressure valve, and I felt lighter than I'd known in years. It was the first time I'd experienced physical changes that carried into my life, and I wanted to know why.

This sparked a curiosity within, and I buried my head in textbooks, searching for answers—what I found absolutely blew my mind! Just learning that the speech centres of the brain can go offline in response to trauma made me question why talking therapy was favoured by traditional healthcare when our own neuroscience and physiology were showing us something different!

I started exploring body-based healing practices like somatic therapy and nervous system regulation techniques, which led to me hiring my first coach. With the right tools and support in place, I slowly began unpicking the tapestry of my life and weaving it back together again.

Within a short space of time, I saw huge shifts, not just in my well-being, but in every area of my life. Whilst this was exciting, it also exposed a painful divide between the person I was becoming and the career that was once a dream.

Working on the frontline comes with a strong survival instinct to belong, after all, our lives depend on each other, and I thought I'd be laughed out of the police station for sharing my truth. I knew the power of authenticity, that it would push some away and pull others closer, which is where history and destiny collide for me.

After the death of my mum, an old childhood fear of abandonment had raised its head, which started a battle between being true to myself and the fear of loss. So, whilst I longed for personal freedom, I believed this came at the cost of my career and the relationships within. I wasn't yet ready to let go, but the more I silenced my voice, the more divided I felt.

In 2023, I transferred to a new force for a fresh start, and from the moment I walked through the door, I knew this was going to be a very different experience. Whilst it was definitely still the police, the culture was different, and I felt I could be more of myself without the constant fear of judgement.

But in a cruel twist of fate, I then lost my sister in tragic circumstances. It felt like history repeating itself, and once again, the joy and freedom I'd just begun to reclaim was overshadowed by immense grief.

In contrast to my mum's death, I stepped away from work and sat in the raw depths of grief in real time. Here, the integrity of the inner work I'd been navigating really began to shine through, and whilst it didn't make the situation any less painful, it helped me find the internal resilience to withstand the fall.

Instead of distracting myself and keeping busy, I had tools such as breathwork to keep me present, honest, and grounded. Instead of avoiding difficult feelings, I knew how to regulate my nervous system during intense emotions. Instead of pretending I was fine, I'd developed the somatic awareness to understand and meet my innermost needs.

If anything, the loss of my sister only deepened my trust in the somatic pathway and working with the body to heal trauma. Which, in turn, encouraged me to lean into my authenticity and start facing the fears keeping me quiet and small. Life suddenly carried a sense of urgency, a drive to fill that 'blank page' with a legacy to be proud of, which meant telling myself the truth.

I knew my policing career had been over since the challenges I'd faced in 2022, but I'd been clinging on tightly after going through so much loss. Whilst moving to a new force had been a healing experience, it had simply delayed the inevitable.

I was starting to realise how deeply intertwined my identity was with my role as a police officer and that separating the two wasn't going to be easy. I knew I could play it safe and stay in the police with a successful career ahead of me, but a voice within told me it was time to start letting go. Whilst finally acknowledging the truth was liberating, it opened up new levels of fear.

I began questioning why I'd walk away from financial security, especially coming from humble roots. Why give up status and responsibility to start over? Why throw away something I'd worked so hard for? What if I failed and ended up with nothing—who would support me then? And who actually was I without the uniform, anyway?

Feeling overwhelmed, I tried to delay the decision by sharing the somatic therapy and nervous system work I'd been doing from a frontline perspective, hoping to blend both worlds. I knew the value it could offer my colleagues, but the reality of inspiring change within a large organisation, like the police, proved more challenging than I thought—ultimately becoming the final push for me to hand in my badge.

Whilst most people were supportive of my decision, I was also met with comments like "Well, if you don't enjoy it" and "Well, if it's not what you thought"—if only it was that simple! I had many reasons for leaving the police and they hadn't made the list.

On a soul level, I was leaving for the same reason I'd joined—to become the person a younger version of myself needed during her darkest times. Growing up, I'd faced some pretty heavy experiences that left me wondering who was there to protect me. In joining the police, I became that person; she was tough, strong, and resilient—she made my inner child feel safe.

But now the girl writing a goodbye letter to her family, the girl letting go of her dreams—she needed me too, needed me to become the safety net that would've softened her fall.

Whilst I couldn't change the past, I could use my experience to help the emergency services become a better place, which could only happen from the outside. And so, letting go of the uniform that had once been my armour became my greatest act of strength.

Walking out the gates for the final time, my heart was heavy yet immensely proud. I wasn't quite sure where I was headed, but I understood the growth from this experience was an important part of my evolution. Life was taking me in a different direction and I'd answered the call, but that didn't mean the path forward was an easy one.

I struggled to adjust to life outside the police and the structure it provided. Although I never questioned my decision to leave, I felt like a failure without the uniform to hide behind. Old habits crept in, and I compensated by chasing goals, grasping at the external world to soothe that internal fear of not being enough.

I quickly found myself in burnout, which was a wake-up call. It was clear I could no longer sustain the same 'masculine' energy that was once my default—a testament to the work I'd done. It led me to the realisation that I needed less in life, not more. So, I stripped it all back and, for the first time, in a lifetime, gave myself permission to rest.

I was hit by a wave of exhaustion that scared me. I tried to fight back but couldn't find the strength. I was left with no other option but to let go and allow myself to sit in stillness, which turned out to be an incredible gift. It gave me space to digest the last six years—a lot had gone down, and I'd never really stopped to absorb the impact.

I wondered: What if I wasn't lazy or going backwards? What if this exhaustion was my body coming out of survival mode, that my only job now was to be in the present moment and allow old cycles to complete? I decided to trust my intuition on this, which was guiding me to honour the natural flow and wisdom of life.

It had never occurred to let life unfold organically, on its own timelines. I'd always been two steps ahead, lining everything up for the best shot at success. Yet all I'd been doing was trying to force growth, which is like trying to prise open a flower before it's ready to bloom. Over time, I began to see the beauty in surrender and allowing chapters to close before starting a new book.

It struck me how this retreat inward had been the final integration piece between the person I used to be and who I was yet to become—the weaving together of all parts. And as I found the centre point, I was met with this fierce, yet nurturing strength... deep roots, warm heart, curious mind. There was a real sense of closure on this painful period of life, and I was ready to step out into the world again.

The time I'd spent on pause had served another purpose, in that I'd been given space to contemplate my future and what I was here to do. It was clear I had a deep connection to the police and a drive to help those in service, as well as a passion to share the tools that helped me through some of the most challenging days of my life.

So, one of the first things I did when I stepped out of this bubble was to qualify in somatic breathwork, which deepened my skills in working with the body and nervous system to navigate stress, anxiety, burnout, and trauma. Although this practice came with ease, it was always part of a broader plan.

I held a vision that honoured my roots but left me questioning my sanity—I saw a way to hone these tools, make them my own, and take them to the heart of public services, addressing the unique challenges within.

With only my intuition pushing me forward (I've learned to trust this inner voice), I set up Healing Blue Hearts. It's my company providing somatic education, nervous system health, and breathwork to frontline workers, public service professionals, and beyond.

Not only was this a deep calling, it was a beautiful way to keep my sister's memory alive, given her passion for nursing that was cut short with her passing. My work as the founder and CEO of Healing Blue Hearts is to carry forward the light of those I've lost and offer hope to those still finding their way!

With any transformation, it's tempting to be swept away by the 'happy endings' and gloss over the true nature of our path. We often hear people declare painful life experiences as 'the best thing that ever happened to them'—whilst this is admirable, I think the raw beauty and deeper nuances of our story can become lost when we speak only from a place of hindsight.

I find it more liberating to own the truth of my experiences—they weren't the best thing to ever happen to me, and they never will be. But the way I've stepped forward and taken responsibility for my healing, the way I've turned my pain into my purpose... captures the essence of my transformation in a way that no smiling 'after' photo ever could.

Because there was a time I was at war with myself.

There was a lifetime of being told I was too sensitive, too emotional, too deep (things that were actually incredible gifts) had made me feel that I was somewhat lacking. It left me looking for others to love the parts of me I couldn't love myself, looking for permission on who I could be.

Yet the world was simply a mirror, reflecting back at me all the places where I wasn't yet free.

When the need to belong holds us in bondage, authenticity has the power to set us free. By stripping ourselves bare and returning to our roots, we stand in the truth of who we really are. It's not that we become immune to the fear of rejection, judgement, or abandonment; we simply don't allow it to define our worth—we learn how to lead from within.

Now, the parts of me once hidden in the dark are alive within these pages, shining brightly for the world to see.

**SCAN TO MEET ABBIE**

# REESA MORALA

## GENERATIONAL TRAUMA,
## PARENTIFICATION & DESIRE

My name is Reesa, and I live a thriving and fulfilled life. I've been with my partner for 16 years. I'm a mother of two. I'm a marriage and family therapist, and I'm a successful business owner. But it hasn't always been this way...

It was an unexpected and unwanted pregnancy, a fact they never let me forget, to a mother who was in her first year of college and a father 18 years her senior just finishing his third marriage. I was one of two in the womb, but only one of us lived.

My mother, to this day, will tell you my twin died because it was "God's punishment" for having a baby out of wedlock. So, she was insistent that my father marry her. Now, looking back on it, I see how so much of that mindset set the tone for my upbringing. A mindset that sin was to be punished, and punished severely.

The irony of it all is that it was a one-way street. If I walked in on my father doing drugs with his friends, I was the one punished for going where I wasn't supposed to be. If I walked in on my mother giving my father a blowjob, I was shamed for not knocking because I "should have known better." If there wasn't food to eat and I had to fend for myself, I was chastised for how unhealthy I was eating and how much weight I had put on. Much like a Taylor Swift song, the message that stuck at the core of it all: I was the problem. It was me.

Although both of my parents went about handling their own insecurities in very different ways, I believe the end goal was the same. And that goal was to be in their comfort zones, at all costs. Looking outward at how everyone else had failed them was much easier and far too natural than the alternative.

My father has a short temper, and it is not abnormal for him to choke a child or use the belt to do his dirty work and let you know all the ways you have erred. My mother has victimhood perfected down to an art with contemptuous words, tear-filled eyes, and responsibility-taking—a foreign concept.

Remember that mindset? Now that I'm grown, I can see the through lines of how much "Godly fear" was at play in much of my childhood. But back then, it was just the normal way of life.

Here's what I mean… I was raised in the Pentecostal church system. The speaking in tongues and punishment by death based on the severity of your sin. This was and is the rationale for much of what I experienced, which I now know, fortified the layers of invalidation for the trauma I endured.

When I experienced a beating from my father, it was not to be questioned. He was, after all, the head of the household, just as the Bible says he should be. Instead, the question ought to be, what did I do to deserve this?

What sin did I commit that warranted choking?

How did I fail?

Because that was the only logical rationale. I became an expert at self-criticism and analyzing all of the ways I could and, more importantly, would fail.

And sex?! That was the pinnacle topic of ways I could fail. As you might recall, the punishment for that sex out of wedlock was the death of a child. That shame was pervasively passed down. Sex was a means to bring about children and was meant for only man and wife. Not pleasure.

Masturbation = hell.

Oral = hell.

Same sex = hell.

Open relationships = hell.

Anything other than penis to vagina = hell.

Using that lens, now it makes sense, right? It was much easier to punish a child for not knocking and walking in on a blowjob than to admit you were committing a sin. The layer of shame was thick. So much so, in my family, we didn't even talk about sex. The birds and bees conversation I got consisted of listening to Christian (more ways you could be in sin if you were not abstinent until marriage) cassette tapes that both my mother and myself pretended to tune out/fall asleep to because we both wanted to be anywhere but there.

Avoidance was better than talking about the construct of shame and normalizing. In fact, when I provided feedback to my mother, as an adult, about our birds and bees conversation and the areas of improvement, what she heard was, "That didn't work," and took it as the green light to not have any conversations about it with my younger siblings.

I think it was that avoidance that fueled much of the emotional abuse from both my parents. Again, why take responsibility for a mistake, apologize, or accept influence when it was so much easier to put the blame on a child with no voice? No voice, because that, too, was a sin. Instead, they called it "talking back" because then it was punishable.

Admission would mean there was a fault, and the fault was a sin. The fight against being seen as a sinner was so strong that they seemed to miss that it came at the expense of their children's health and well-being. Sharing emotions was labeled as "dramatic" and expressing pain as a "weakness."

But shh. These are not things we speak of. Even to this day. The mere fact that I'm sharing my story with you today is a direct violation of that code and facade. We continued to go to church, every Sunday, and show the world how good of Christians we were.

This was my life... and it was all that I knew. So, I had to figure out how to survive.

As a form of protection I learned how to people-please. In my world, it was too dangerous to have a voice or an identity. I became great at being a chameleon. It was safer. And I got SO good at playing my role. I was a standout volunteer at church; they even had me teaching Sunday School when I was in high school because I was a model student. Any normal, teenage sexual curiosity or thoughts—I knew how to suppress because I couldn't "let the devil win." I cooked and cleaned because my parents "didn't have the energy for us." I got straight A's and was top of my class, to be one less thing they had to worry about.

I became my mother's biggest fan by telling her how good of a parent she was and validating her emotions because it was better than the verbal lashing when she felt insecure. My thoughts and emotions were not my own. They were in service to the cause.

And when I failed to play my role, I was reminded, times three, about how much of a disappointing excuse of a person I was. The third voice was my own. My experience honed my inner critic. The self-flagellation became one more skill that I was amazing at.

And that fact was incredibly lonely and isolating. After all, this was only happening to me because that day I wasn't perfect enough. Why would I share my failure with anyone? I got enough shame at home. Why would anyone want to be around a disappointment? I was very familiar with my lack of worth.

Perfectionism was my savior. Perfection meant safety. Perfection meant acceptance. Perfection meant worth. Perfection meant love.

These maladaptive beliefs became so ingrained that I found it easy to slip into a similar construct that my parents were in. Things were happening to me. Punishment for my failings. I had no control.

I vividly remember begging my mother for a reprieve from her judgment and criticisms of my "out of wedlock" sex when trying to share with her my fear over abnormal cells being found during my latest pap smear because I already knew that it was my judgment for my sin. A sin that I wasn't a virgin anymore. It was happening to me. Even a health issue.

When my three-month-old child stopped eating, I racked my brain for what sin I was paying for. Was it because my partner and I had gotten married in secret? Was it because we looked at a Kama Sutra book that was risque and adventurous? Was it because we got into an argument about our differing stances on masturbation and even dared to think about it? Was it because we hadn't been going to church? Was it because I was speeding on the freeway? It was happening to me and now impacting my child. Even a health issue.

While others may find a passing down of recipes or clothes, heirlooms, or wealth, my acquisitions were invisible. Avoidance, shame, guilt, criticism, contempt, violence, and an external locus of control was my generational inheritance. You would never have been able to tell by looking at me. That was a point of pride for a long time.

I found myself at a place where I had a choice to make. The most comfortable and easiest decision would be to stay within the chaos—throw my hands up in defeat because these are things happening to me, and I had no control. Or choose the unknown of change.

Change I wasn't familiar with.

Change I didn't know how to achieve.

Change that would mean an upheaval of everything that I knew and had been taught.

Change that would eventually mean a distancing from my family of origin that culturally and societally would be frowned upon.

That was one of the scariest decisions of my life thus far. That period was one of the most uncomfortable moments in my body. This choice is still one that I have to make and battle on a daily basis, to this day. For me, that is the only way to break that generational trauma. It's taking back control of my life and making a choice. A choice to choose knowledge. A choice to seek help. A choice for something better for my children.

It was not an overnight switch. There was no magical cure. It has been a constant and winding journey.

My healing started with my undergraduate therapist who became the first person to ever ask me what my beliefs were. Not what I was taught. Not what I was shown. But me. What did I believe in and why? She was the first person to ever ask me what my needs were, without ulterior motives. But simply to provide a space for my voice. She was the first person to validate the hurt and the pain, without using it to demean or laud over me. She was the first person to challenge me to explore my identity, separate from my parents. Separate from the church. An identity that was authentic to my values and to know that my values had worth.

My healing continued as I went through my graduate program to pay it forward in helping others. I began to learn about what abuse looked like. I discovered knowledge of healthy family systems and generational trauma. I was challenged to look at my own hangups and constructs.

My professors encouraged me to deeply understand what I might bring into the therapy room based on my own wounds. It became a space that taught me how to offer myself grace and unconditional positive regard, just as I would my clients.

Grace to learn that what I went through wasn't "normal" or my "punishment" for sin. That the treatment and experiences weren't something I deserved or had earned for my lack of perfectionism. They were impossible standards that were set forth and designed to support my failing. Designed to elicit subordination. Designed to ensure my conformity to the generational cycles that came before me.

Grace to accept that in many of those moments, I was a child. I was brought into this world, not by my own choice. I was a child learning to be in the world for the first time. There were limits to what I was capable of being exposed to based on my developmentally appropriate dependence.

Grace to finally say, I am a human being. A human who is prone to fickle failings just like the next person.

These ideas finally had space to form. Their blooming, though, came with the birth of my own children. Here's what I mean... Remember my child who stopped eating? Let me give you some more context.

When my first child was born, by three weeks old, I knew something was wrong. I took him to the doctor and told her he was constantly "spitting up" larger volumes that seemed more like vomiting. She shooed me away and told me I was "overreacting" and "just a first-time mom." There was that narrative—a person of authority was telling me it was a "me" problem. So, I quieted the voice that something was wrong.

By 3 months old, he stopped eating altogether. Not from the breast. Not from a bottle. Not breastmilk. Not formula. He wasn't eating. He was hungry, but he wasn't eating. A basic need. I couldn't provide for him. My sole job was to keep him alive, and I couldn't get him to eat. There was that narrative, again—I'm the problem.

I felt so desperate that I broke down and called my mother. Because that was what I knew, right? I lamented and opened up, one more time. Maybe this time, I'd get a "mother." My child was facing a life-or-death issue. This was worth it, right?

"It's not that hard, Reesa. I was able to feed all three of you. I would just put you on the bed and pop my boob out and shove it in your mouth, and you'd eat. It's not that hard, Reesa. You're just not doing it right."

It was at that moment that I became my own mother.

Driving north on the I-15 freeway, I made a choice. It was time to grieve for the mother I was not going to get from anyone else. It was time for me to show up. To be the mother I deserved to myself. That my child needed me to be. That my child was worth it.

I went back to the doctor's, and I demanded they start listening. I spoke up for the child in my arms. I spoke up for my inner child. It was not my doing. It was not because of a failing. Something was wrong.

That became the first of many opportunities to start teasing out the inner critic. Start differentiating the voice of the generations before me from my own. The instinct was strong, but I knew I was capable. That fact cemented each time I showed up.

I showed myself that, as a parent, I may not have known what to do (after all, I didn't have a model or a manual), but I had the capability to learn. I had the motivation to seek out help from others who had knowledge, experience, and training to share. I had the power to take responsibility for the human mistakes that I made and the humility to ask for forgiveness—even from my child.

It was one foot in front of the other. It was working through the instinct for just surviving and moving into thriving. It was cultivating, for myself, my worth and my value. Not defined by others.

I had a choice.

Yes, there are things that I have and will continue to encounter that are out of my control.

So, it has become a fine dance of increasing my awareness of the things that I can control and what I cannot. Choosing to move out of the comfort of saying it is happening to me because of the cards I was or wasn't dealt is my choice.

A daily choice.

One that my spouse is worth it.

My children are worth it.

And that girl on the left is worth it.

SCAN TO MEET REESA

# BERENICE BRITO

## DIVORCE, CO-PARENTING & HARMONY

As the laughter and chatter swirled around the room, there I was—the girl on the left—always perched on the outskirts of my own life, a silent observer in a world that felt endlessly vibrant yet impossibly distant. While everyone else danced in the spotlight, I clung to the shadows, grappling with the ache of isolation that whispered, "You don't belong here." Little did I know this solitude would catalyze the transformation I never knew I needed.

I spent most of my life feeling like an outsider, the odd duck out, never quite fitting in. I was sweet and caring, and people generally liked me, but I struggled to deepen relationships. I was friendly enough to form surface-level connections, but something in me—something I couldn't even put into words—kept me from getting too close. I believed I was different, too different to find my place.

I didn't realize then that I didn't need someone just like me to feel connected. I needed to find "me." The real me, hidden under layers of self-protection, fear, and the beliefs I had absorbed throughout my life. It wasn't sameness that would allow me to build genuine relationships—it was authenticity in myself and others. But back then, I didn't know how to be authentic. I didn't know who I was beneath the mask.

I grew up in a world where love was conditional, validation had to be earned, and I learned early on that I could only depend on myself.

My father had a lot of narcissistic traits and was emotionally unavailable, unable to love and prioritize me in the way I desperately needed. His words still echo in my mind: "Don't ask me, I don't like to tell you 'no.'" It was easier for him, a throwaway comment, but to me, it was a reminder that I couldn't rely on him.

My needs were inconvenient, my desires unimportant.

And then there was my mother.

She worked tirelessly—over 60 hours a week—to ensure we had what we needed. But her absence left a void that no material provision could fill. My mother grew up without parents, an orphan raised in boarding schools. She never learned to receive love, nor did she learn to give it. I was raised by nannies and caregivers who were present physically but absent emotionally.

They didn't understand me, didn't try to. They were too busy doing what "they" thought was important, leaving me alone to navigate my emotions and my growing sense of unworthiness. I had plenty of freedom and miserably lacked adult supervision.

I learned from an early age that no one had my back. If I wanted something done, I had to do it myself. So, I became fiercely independent—not out of strength, but out of fear. I was afraid to ask for help, afraid to lean on anyone, afraid to trust that someone would be there for me. I hid. I played small. I stayed in the shadows.

And so, I moved through life with my head down, focused only on my own steps, too afraid to look up and be seen. I was terrified that if people really saw me, they wouldn't like what they found. My own family did not value or prioritize me; why would others?

So, I wore a mask—the mask of the good girl, the hard worker, the one who didn't need anything from anyone. It was easier that way. Less painful—or so I thought.

But this mask came at a cost. I disconnected from myself, and I disconnected from the world around me. I pushed through life, doing everything I was "supposed" to do, always striving for perfection but never stopping to live truly. I was existing and surviving, not thriving.

And then, when I got older, came my relationships. I dated men who mirrored the same emotional unavailability I had grown up with. Men who couldn't give me the love and connection I craved. Men who, like me, didn't know how to be vulnerable. I stayed in relationships that felt familiar in their dysfunction because I believed this was all love was meant to be—something you endured, not thrived in.

I thought I was broken. I thought this was just who I was, that I was destined to live a life half-lived, always looking in from the outside, never fully part of anything.

But life has a way of pushing us to the brink before it shows us the light. And for me, that push came in the form of motherhood.

Even though I've loved babies since my tender years spent in hospital nurseries while my mom was on shift, I thought being a mother was not in the cards for me. For the longest time, I kept thinking I was not good enough or worthy of being a mom. This way of thinking was the first thing I pivoted by reframing it as "if I was meant to be a mother, it would happen somehow..."

A few weeks later, an unusual feeling in my pelvis alerted me that things had changed. When I found out I was pregnant, something shifted in me. I was going to be a mother. I was going to have a child who would look to me for guidance, love, and security. And in that moment, I knew I couldn't let my son grow up with the same limiting beliefs that had defined my life. I couldn't let him inherit my fears, my insecurities, my patterns of self-sabotage. I had to change not just for me but for him.

Motherhood became my catalyst for transformation. It forced me to confront the shadows I had been living in for so long. I couldn't hide anymore. I had to step into the light, into my entire self, because my son needed me to be whole. He needed me to be the example of what a life lived in authenticity, love, and connection looked like.

Being pregnant was the highlight of my life thus far. I had so much love for that little human growing inside of me. I would tell him daily how much I loved him—and I still do it today! Glimpsing at what a happy life looks like made me realize I had been settling instead of chasing my happiness. For the first time, I had proof that I was more than worthy. I was a powerhouse capable of love and bliss.

And yet, things did not magically become better. I had never felt more alone. After my son was born, I had this little baby to care for and no one to help me. I put my son first. I did everything possible for him and let myself stay in the background. I disregarded my own needs to provide for him.

I stopped taking care of myself.

And since I was looking for ways of being happier, I found the easy pleasure of eating. Sweets became one of my go-to foods, and I gained a lot of weight.

One day, I looked at myself in a mirror and did not recognize the woman staring back at me. She was older, but her eyes did not reflect knowledge. They mirrored only sadness back to me. I had my North Star, my son, and yet I could not bask in happiness because I was still living an empty life.

I had learned to be a people pleaser, and that conditioning continued. I would give my son the clothes off my back—and yet, what would that teach him?

There is nothing wrong with giving, as long as we do it consciously with a hefty regard for our well-being. When we care for ourselves, we give from a place of abundance instead of dwindling resources.

I knew what I wanted and was confident I wasn't getting it by doing the same things I had always done. The answers would not be found in the avoiding or numbing. I was still disconnected and escaping instead of actively doing things to change my reality.

My vice was generally safe in the grand scheme of things: I read a lot—365 books in one year was my record! I did everything while reading and needed the excitement of those stories to keep me going. It's heartbreaking to look back and see that I did not enjoy my life enough for it to suffice as motivation.

I cleaned my house listening to Audible. I did the same while driving to work. I would start a shift already looking forward to my break to get a few pages in. I needed to read that extra chapter so I could have the strength to push on and make it home okay.

Books saved me. Even though they were a coping mechanism, they provided the awakening I needed. By showing me that, like my heroines, I had everything inside of me to be victorious even though I had a lot of baggage. This certainty allowed me to go on and fight to change the things I did not appreciate about my status quo.

At the same time, my body was breaking down. My health was deteriorating in front of my eyes. My hands, the essential tools that enable us to connect with the world around us in profound and multifaceted ways, were cracking and splitting. The skin that should allow me to interact through touch was riddled with immeasurable pain that prevented me from even holding my son. In my world, pain signifies "pay attention inward now," and so I did.

I realized that the disconnection inside, the one to myself, was preventing me from living the full life I wanted. But change is never easy, and the path to healing is often messy. I made mistakes along the way. I stumbled. I fell back into old patterns. But I was determined. I began doing the inner, deep, soul-searching work I now help my clients do.

I started by looking at my beliefs—those deeply ingrained stories that had shaped my life. I realized that so much of my beliefs about myself weren't true. I wasn't unworthy. I wasn't broken. I wasn't destined to live in the shadows. These were just lies I had been telling myself for years, lies that had been passed down to me from my family, from society, from my own experiences of pain and rejection.

Slowly, I began to unravel those lies. I started to see myself for who I truly was—strong, capable, worthy of love. I learned to forgive myself for the mistakes I had made, for the years I had spent hiding, for the relationships I had stayed in out of fear. I learned to let go of the past and focus on creating my desired future.

Despite commonly being seen as getting over or rid of something, letting go means letting things happen. Imagine yourself holding a ball underwater. Letting it go does not make it disappear. It allows the ball to continue existing without your influence. It also frees your hands so that you can perform better strokes and swim further. Knowing how it feels to try and swim while holding the ball provides insight that can be useful when deciding if you want to hold on to it again or to leave it aside as you continue without it.

Knowledge strengthens our power of choice and allows us to make informed decisions.

As a source of knowledge, we can look at the past as a guide instead of a determining factor in our fates. Letting go of what once was and stepping into our futures with the information we gathered from living through it.

Even though I've spent my entire life scared of being alone like my mother, I chose to leave my husband and venture out on my own. A consequence of realizing that he would never be the support I craved. The awareness that I was lonely, even if I was not alone on paper, motivated me to take action.

I faced many challenges. Life kept on "life-ing" and throwing me curveballs.

But as I moved past each obstacle, I felt stronger. I had more tools to maneuver the bad and incredible techniques to expand the good.

As I did this work, I started to see changes in my life. My relationships improved, not just with others but with myself. I stopped seeking validation from the outside and started giving it to myself. I learned to trust myself, listen to my intuition, and honor my needs and desires. I began to fall in love with myself.

I learned that, even though a part of me, my scars do not define me. I'm much more than I've ever given myself credit for. I am a work in progress...

I used to be a perfectionist and strive for the unachievable. I've learned to create bite-size goals to move me toward my desires. Perfection is not achievable in this earthly existence, yet I can always create the most perfect version of reality for me. And it is always beautifully flawed and amazing!

In my journey, I distanced myself from the people disrupting my well-being. I created the space to heal myself, and because of it, my relationships with them flourished. Now, I understand that my parents did not know better and that they did the best they could—even if it was not up to my expectations.

I've come to realize that my ex-husband is entrenched in a place of pain and that it is my choice how much I allow his feelings to affect me. Boundaries are an essential piece of this quest. I've also learned that acknowledging his hurt enables me to combat it with compassion. And this change in myself has allowed us to move into an effective co-parenting dynamic of working as a team for the sake of our son.

More than that, I discovered that being bare-bones and honest with a real partner is paramount. I allow my man to see my scars' darkness and radiance at full blast. I've unmasked all my demons, weaknesses, and perceived failures because I want him to see the full spectrum of me.

Since I've lived most of my life masking, being embraced as I am is the epitome of acceptance. In doing so, I remove the fear of being abandoned, and whenever a thought of "what he will think of me now" pops up, I'm confident we will weather it together. It allows me to be brave and talk to him about it because I know he views me differently than I see myself. He values me despite my misgivings. He knows who I truly am and is proud to be with me.

When we talk it over, things that would make me doubt myself, make myself small, or even "punish" myself for—even if only with words—are not as big of a deal as they initially seem inside my head.

I have quieted down that inner critic that causes so much pain and distrust. The one that always makes the bad seem insurmountable. And by doing so, I have opened up space for compassion to extend to myself.

I accept all parts of myself: the abandoned little girl. The disconnected woman. The resilient mother who is becoming the best version of herself. I am many. I am one. I wear many hats and am deeply connected to the souls in my world.

When we choose someone to love, we are to embrace the entirety of who they are with all that being us encompasses. The freedom of living openly in our truth is crucial for a healthy relationship. Our vulnerability opens up theirs and disarms their defensiveness. It allows us to connect at a deeper level.

We are all different people, yet we all have so much to share of ourselves with those around us. We grow stronger by understanding our differences and recognizing others' points of view. There is so much knowledge to be gained when you enter someone else's world and see life through their eyes.

I've always believed that the best way of learning is by witnessing how other people do things. And we do that in our formational years by modeling those around us. The problem is that most of us did not have good examples to follow. The beauty of life is that it's not too late to choose who you want to model after. Modeling excellence helps us to up-level how we go through life. A simple and effective way to start this process is by looking around us and finding characteristics in our loved ones that we admire.

If we are messy and our partner isn't, instead of getting upset that they want us to clean up, take it as an empowering new skill that we can learn to improve ourselves. If we are shy and quiet, using their outgoing nature can provide us comfort and a stronger foundation for ourselves to speak up.

An epic relationship ensues when both partners bring their imperfect parts to the mix and learn to grow together. We all have our strengths and weaknesses... One provides us the resilience to evolve, and the other brings up the things we should work on.

Carl Jung said that our partners are chosen to hash out all the unhealed parts of us and that until we make the unconscious conscious, it directs our lives, and we call it fate. One reason relationships are so meaningful is that they help us grow by bringing to light things to work on. I am not what happened to me but what I choose to become.

My past unfulfilling or even toxic relationships are a part of my story.

They have taught me to become a better participant in my current relationships.

My intentional actions reflect my inner state, so I carefully tend to my heart, mind, and soul.

By showing care for those three aspects of me, I manifest the physical reality I most resonate with. I no longer run out of energy or feel depleted. I have a love tank that is always full. I've learned to give from overflow, so I'm never left empty.

I have made many mistakes, yet I'm proud of how I address them. I live without regrets because I've chosen to use my past as a propelling force to create the future I want.

I also realized that I wasn't alone in this struggle. So many people, especially high-achievers, find themselves in the same place I was—overwhelmed, disconnected, and running on empty.

They think they must keep pushing, striving, and doing more to feel worthy and successful. But the truth is, no amount of external success can fill the void inside if we don't first connect with ourselves.

Through my work as a transformational coach, I now help people do the same inner work that transformed my life.

I help them release the limiting beliefs that are holding them back.

I help them heal their relationships, both with themselves and with others.

I help them create a life that feels complete and meaningful, not just busy.

I want my clients to know that they are not broken. They don't need to be fixed. They are whole, just as they are, and the power to change their lives has always been within them. It's just a matter of tapping into that power, peeling back the layers of fear and self-doubt, and allowing their true selves to emerge.

I help people up-level their relationships so they can love their lives every day. I help them move from surviving to thriving, from feeling stuck in a half-life to living a life they are proud of. And it all starts with the same thing that started my journey—doing the inner work.

The girl on the left, the one who used to cling to the shadows, is no longer afraid to be seen. She is no longer hiding. She has stepped into the light and her full power and lives a life of connection, love, and fulfillment. And now, I'm here to help others do the same.

The journey isn't easy. There will be bumps along the way. You will make mistakes. But those mistakes don't define you. They are simply stepping stones on the path to your true self.

So, if you find yourself stuck in a cycle of busyness, disconnected from your own life, and feeling like you're living on the outskirts of your own joy, know there is a way out. You are not alone. And you don't have to stay in the shadows any longer.

Your dream life is waiting for you, and I'm here to light up your path and guide you toward it. You are worthy of living a full, connected, and joyful life. And the power to create that life has always been within you.

Stop waiting for the next business goal. Stop waiting for the stars to align. You don't have to push through life on your own.

Take a step toward the life you truly want—feeling loved, connected, and at peace.

You don't have to walk this path alone. I'm here to walk it with you. Together, we can create a life that you love.

**SCAN TO MEET BERENICE**

# TAWNY STEPHENS

## GRIEF, ANGER & FINDING LIGHT

Here are some attributes of the woman who got me through the absolute worst two and a half years of my life.

- She was stubborn
- She was angry
- She was really, really angry
- She was protective
- She was in survival mode
- She was fiercely in love with her children
- She was determined
- She was driven
- She was powerless, which made her powerful

She stuffed all of her feelings down deep inside of her, she did it in order to keep functioning when she felt like she had no ability to function.

- She escaped a lot
- She was needy, but she refused to need
- She was spiritually hungry, but she kept God at arm's length
- She was bold
- She was funny
- She was deliberate

She had what felt like 1,000 plates spinning in the air at all times, and if she let one crack of vulnerability in, she *knew* that they would all come crashing down. She truly thought she would never recover if that happened.

* * *

I was married to a really wonderful man, and somewhere along the way, he developed alcoholism. He had signs of addiction in his past that he had overcome. He had a recurring problem with tobacco, which was a constant point of contention throughout our marriage, but when someone was as wonderful as my husband Mike was, I chose to ignore it. He was compassionate and gentle. He was funny. He was just self-deprecating enough to be charming. He loved the arts as much as he loved football; he was always singing.

Everybody who met Mike loved Mike. And for a good 14 years, any little thing that I might find to complain about seemed trivial. For a long time, we coasted through good times and bad times. It was a pretty easy marriage with occasional trivial arguments over seemingly trivial things. Then, when our lives got really hard, he began a quick and steady decline into alcoholism. The change was so subtle that I honestly can't tell you how long the problem existed before I even noticed.

He struggled so much with shame that he hid. He hid the addiction. He hid that and multiple other things from me until he declined so much that he couldn't hide them anymore. When I finally found out, I was livid. That version of me had no grace. That version of me had no understanding. That version of me was pissed. She was ready to leave and ready to start over. I had given everything over to him. I had put all of my trust in him. I had quit working to raise our kids. I had given him my livelihood. I had forfeited my credit and my name. I had given him all of my autonomy, only to find that he was incapable of handling it.

I understand myself a little better now—I have since realized that I am an Enneagram Type 8 (7 wing), and autonomy is, in fact, the biggest treasure I have to give. I trusted him with everything. This meant all the finances and the big decisions, and, ultimately, I trusted him with our lives. This trust was betrayed. I felt utterly helpless and defenseless.

And then I felt alone.

We were not close to family. We had some wonderful friends, but we had slowly isolated from them. There was no longer laughter and singing in the house. There was only this sadness and all of these secrets steeped in shame. I wanted away from that.

I watched him use AA as a crutch to heal "just enough" that he could justify continuing to drink. I watched him sleep through days when he was supposed to be working from home. I saw him fall down flights of stairs and blame them for being slippery from rain. I watched him go through two or three supposed detoxes at home, only to secretly start drinking again within a few weeks.

Through all of this, we had these two small kids who needed us. They needed somebody.

They needed at least one parent.

Suddenly I felt like the only adult. I felt so alone and afraid and heartbroken. In spite of those big feelings, I could not let myself feel those things because I did not feel like I would survive if I let myself truly feel them. So, I just went into anger and escaped instead.

I was happy that the kids didn't seem to notice how much he was changing. I was thankful that he was able to pull himself together long enough to make it to a performance or watch them win an award. Through my very aware filter, though, it was sad because even the good memories they were making with him at the time were tainted for me. I could see the circumstance through adult eyes, and all I could do was hope at the time that they would take the good parts and not see the whole truth around it.

I knew our marriage was over, but I think there was a part of me that honestly believed that Mike and I would get a divorce, and that would be his "rock bottom." That he would snap out of it and go get sober.

I believed that the rest of his family would understand that he really had a problem and not just the parts of the story that he was telling them. That he would come back into our lives as himself again because he hadn't been *him* for a very long time. That he would come back, and I would even get an apology! In my mind, we wouldn't necessarily reconcile and be married again, but I would at least get my friend back, and we could be really good co-parents.

But he didn't have that in him.

He did not have the ability to "snap out of it." He did not have the ability to heal himself. His dad finally agreed to come to town and move him out to his own apartment. The turning point came on Easter Sunday. The kids and I went to a church I hadn't really been to before, and I sat in the back. Size-wise? It was a *mega* church so it was like, the balcony way in the *back back*.

And I wept.

I wept for what we were going through. For what we were losing. For the first time, I let a crack of vulnerability open. It was a prayer without words.

I was utterly and completely hopeless. I had no idea what we were going to do, I just knew I couldn't do it by myself anymore. Mike had been throwing up all day before, that is why he didn't come to church with us. I had checked on him throughout the day because I knew if he couldn't keep anything down, he would start detoxing pretty quickly.

That evening we spoke one last time.

I asked if he needed me to take him to the hospital. He said he was doing a little better and that he was able to go to the gas station and get some Gatorade. I remember telling him (kindly, for the first time in a long time) that I was really worried. That I needed him to hear me while I knew he was sober enough to understand. That he *had* to stop for good. That he really wasn't okay.

I don't remember what he said in response, but I encouraged him to rest.

The next morning when I called to check back in, he wasn't answering his phone. I called several times.

No answer.

Then, I went to wake up my daughter, and she said, "Mom, I had a dream. We were at Dad's house, but it wasn't his house. It was bigger and had a lot of rooms."

And I knew he was gone.

It's funny. We wall our hearts up with anger. We build a fortress to protect ourselves from the pain. But when death arrives? The anger is irrelevant, and only the sadness remains to be dealt with.

What do you do with layers and layers of anger? What do you do with years of hurt and sadness where you've been on a roller coaster every six weeks of thinking you've resolved something just to find another bottle in another hiding spot? What do you do when there's no (sober) I'm sorry?

More importantly, where do you shove all that emotion when you suddenly have two elementary school students who have to process that they won't see their dad again? How do you tell them?

You know, I've heard from some people (some who were close to me, which was quite a shock) who say things like: "You weren't happily married anymore. You separated before he died, so it's not the same level of grief you would be dealing with if you had been happily married still."

Honestly? First of all, fuck those people.

But second of all, I don't even know how to comprehend the fact that I never got to mourn the real version of him. This other version had taken over for so long that I had already been mourning him for years, and *now* I had to deal with the grief of him dying on top of it.

So, you know... That girl? That version of me? She was a real bitch. The one who carried me through those years, she was a real asshole sometimes. And she was mean, on purpose. Very mean.

Because she wanted to hurt his feelings. She wanted to force him to wake up and get help. She wanted him to hurt like she was hurting so that he would realize that he shouldn't do this to himself or us anymore. She wanted him to acknowledge all that she had to do, that she had to step up because he wouldn't (couldn't), and had to go back to work after nine years at home with the kids because he was falling apart. She wanted him to acknowledge what she had put up with and what he had put her through.

I don't like the girl that I was, but I, sure as fuck: Sitting in my life today, remarried, in a house that I pay for, with kids thriving in school and extracurriculars—I, sure as shit, am not going to judge her. Why? Because she fought like hell to scrape out some stability for this family. She did the very best she could do in a very horrible situation.

Maybe it wasn't the best she could do. But she did all she could.

I remember my best friend telling me: "Just survive," and by God if nothing else, I did.

You know, at the end of the day, that is what my children needed. They needed a parent who was willing to survive for them. A parent who was willing to say:

"Life is awful right now. It is absolute and utter shit right now. We are poor. We are angry. We are living with an active alcoholic. We are in the depths of it, but I will not quit. I will not leave you parentless. I will not give up on this shitty life while you still need a parent. I will battle through this life because you deserve to have a mom. I will trudge through this life for you so that you at least know there is someone who loves you more than anybody.

So that you have someone to come to your choir concerts and your plays. Someone to write you notes in your lunch boxes and sit up with you when you're sick. I will be there for you even though I am currently the shittiest version of myself. I will do every inconvenient thing when I already feel like existence is inconvenient enough. I will do it so that you have a parent who does not quit. I will provide whatever I need to provide in order to make sure you can have as normal of a childhood as possible under the circumstances."

A few months later, for my 40th birthday, I treated myself to my first tattoo. It was a line from a poem called "Jesus of the Scars" by Edward Shillito. It reads, "But to our wounds, only God's wounds can speak." Inside the letter are some lines and flecks of yellow to represent the art of kintsugi (where broken objects are put back together with gold, making them even more beautiful than when they were whole). At the front and back of the words are two circles representing stones (biblically, when something significant and holy happens, you would mark the spot with stones).

My experience with Mike's addiction broke me. It showed me the absolute best and worst of myself. And it was not the mighty, all-powerful God who met me in that brokenness, but the scarred and wounded Christ, who overwhelmed me with compassion and showed me how to put one foot in front of the other each day.

About five months after Mike passed, this guy Ace McKay walked into my workplace, shook my hand, and asked about my tattoo. Within the month, "we" were an "us." Then, within the following months, even just as my boyfriend, he was actively parenting the kids and walking with us through the grief process. He has approached loving us with patience and humility, and I could never be grateful enough that God brought him into our lives when we needed him so badly.

I am still angry sometimes. I'm still sad. Especially when I watch the kids excel at something, because Mike's missing it. Ace is an absolute gift to the three of us, but there's a part of them that will always need Dad.

When I take moments like these to reflect on that time, I am proud of the woman I was then, because she did not quit on herself or her kids. She was not content to just give up or accept her fate. She kept moving forward. She was determined to survive.

She was determined to make a better life for her family. She was determined to carve out a space for herself and her kids that they could be proud of. To buy a home. To land her dream job. To make her mark as an artist. She was determined to keep going because she saw a future where those things could be a possibility and she was not content to stay put.

She was not content to wallow.

But she leaned into her anger, to protect herself from the vulnerability.

I believe God allowed the girl that I was to keep him at arm's length for her survival. But I believe he knew what was coming—and he knew she wouldn't be able to keep trying to do it on her own. This was not a salvation moment. I had known the Lord for a long time. But in our relationships with him, I believe he allows us to be as close or as far as we choose. On this day, I believe he reminded me that I needed to be near.

See, God had watched that girl spinning those plates, and he knew they were literally about to burst into shards around her. So, I am grateful for the anger that carried that girl through the first two years, but I am also grateful for the vulnerability that she allowed to come through so that God could finally take over.

I've done my best every day for the past six and a half years to continue letting her anger go. God and I continue to chisel it away together. Ace helps.

Grief is a tricky bitch.

It is not reserved for people who are in happy marriages. I'm grateful for the strength of the woman who walked me through losing my love over a painful, years-long process, piece by piece. If I could tell her anything, I would tell her that I'm good. I'm safe. She doesn't have to protect me anymore.

I'm okay.

She can rest.

Yes, I'm more vulnerable now than I ever was, and some days that scares the shit out of me. But if you're willing to let the vulnerability in, you can also let in the light; and the light is beautiful.

**SCAN TO MEET TAWNY**

# COACH DR. WU
## PTSD, WOUNDED WARRIOR & HEALER

In January 2020, I wrote a letter to my 27-year-old self—my younger, soldier self. It had taken me decades to realize that she, my newly married young physician self, had been left behind in the desert for over 30 years, forgotten and abandoned by the one person who should have cherished her most: me.

She is my girl on the left.

She is the girl that was left behind... by me.

This is a glimpse into my ongoing healing journey—a journey of reaching back through the years to find, embrace, and reintegrate all the parts of myself I left along the way.

A journey to heal and become whole once again.

It started on a day I'll never forget: Father's Day, June 17, 1990. That was the day my beloved BaBa died of terminal cancer. Only four weeks earlier, we'd found out why he'd been suffering from intermittent fevers and persistent back pain. All that time, he'd been using Tiger Balm to try to ease his aches, but by then, cancer had already hollowed out his bones.

Within a month of his diagnosis, he slipped into a coma and never woke up. A piece of my heart felt lost and seemed to vanish with him, leaving an empty spot. At 27, I felt as if my foundation in this world had shifted. There was an emptiness in me I couldn't name, a quiet, gaping void.

I was grateful, though, for two brief moments of solace—two times when I let myself collapse into sobs in my husband's arms. We both loved him so much, the weight of our shared grief breaking the dam of our composure. I felt a glimmer of hope thinking, maybe I could survive this loss. Maybe I could feel secure in this world again, even without my BaBa.

Unfortunately, just a few days after the funeral, duty called. I was sent to basic training for Army officers and trauma management. I was on active duty, and the military waits for no one's grieving process. Without warning, I was whisked away from my family and thrown into the harsh, regimented environment of training—a place with little room for personal sorrow.

This stalled my natural healing process. I buried my grief beneath the rigid discipline and structure of my new role. There was no time or space to grieve, no time to be a daughter who had just lost her father. My role was to heal others, not myself.

Thankfully, I did find purpose in my work as a General Medical Officer at an army base. I became the family physician for a small military base, serving as a caretaker for my own tiny "village." I hung my diplomas and certificates on the walls, claiming this place as my professional home.

I wanted to believe I'd found a place of stability and meaning, something I could hold onto. I told myself this was enough, that I could continue on. But that was short-lived.

A few short months later, I was deployed to a war zone in the Middle East. I replaced the spot of a more seasoned physician who talked their way out of active duty. My orders came unexpectedly, and I knew that resisting wasn't an option. So, I packed up my duffel bag and got on an airplane in the middle of the night. I joined a new medical unit and met a new group of strangers.

Little did we know how dangerous it was to send a grieving young woman into a war zone: before she had any time, space, or help to start to heal... I prayed as I boarded the final plane: "Please, God, watch over this land that I love. Watch over my family and friends. I hope I get to touch this land again, alive."

In that moment, as the plane lifted off, I felt a piece of myself stay behind. I felt as if I were saying goodbye to the young, hopeful woman who had once believed life would unfold predictably. I was no longer the new physician or newlywed, but someone completely brand new to me. I was Captain Wu, MD, stepping into the shadows of war.

I served through Operation Desert Shield and Operation Desert Storm in the Gulf War. The eight months that followed could fill a book on their own. In a war zone, days and nights bleed into each other. It's easy to lose any sense of time or place, and eventually, you can even lose track of yourself.

Each day, I woke up and went through the motions, fulfilling my duty as a physician, treating injuries, comforting the wounded, and ignoring the pain inside me. I thought if I just kept moving, I could leave it all behind. I told myself I would be fine once I returned home.

But when I finally flew back in April 1991, landing on American soil again, "home" felt foreign to me. I turned in my gear—pistol, gas mask, and the rough, worn cot that had been my bed for months—and boarded another plane back to civilian life, where I thought I'd finally find peace. We all thought I was safe now… NOT!

Something integral had changed in me, something I couldn't identify or understand. I didn't feel safe. I had felt so isolated and exiled when I was sent away from my family and my own grieving healing process. I didn't feel at home anymore.

I tried to reconnect with my life by slipping one of my favorite cassette tapes that I had created for my deployment into the car stereo. But somehow, I lost track of three hours. To this day, I don't recall where I drove. Now, I know what actually happened to my nervous system.

My husband, my civilian anchor, had suffered emotionally in his own way. He'd received no word from the military about my safety, no updates or support while I was deployed.

He was left completely in the dark, with only his worst fears and worries for company.

He was powerless to help me, with no timelines for my return.

While I was gone, he literally worked and slept at the hospital most nights, unable to go home to an empty house.

In the loneliness of one of those early nights back, I felt so overwhelmed by despair and isolation that I experienced thoughts of leaving this world. I faced a darkness so consuming that I wondered about it. By God's merciful grace, I simply cried myself to sleep. When I awoke, I shared my darkest thoughts with my husband and eventually with my commander, who arranged for me to see an Army counselor.

I'll never forget my session with the psychiatrist—a man who challenged me and exclaimed pompously, "You would never kill yourself!" That arrogance and total lack of empathy shocked and infuriated me! I felt so unseen, so dismissed.

For a fleeting moment, I felt tempted to prove him wrong. I thought, "Out of spite, maybe I should off myself, just to get him in trouble!" Thankfully, a voice within held me back and talked sense into my rebellious instincts. I pray to this day that he learned compassion and did not wound any other souls with suicidal thoughts in the way he wounded me.

Decades passed, and I asked my former husband: "How did I act, after the war?" He told me, "You returned as a different person. You seemed distant, closed, and just *so* different." I didn't know how to respond, because I didn't fully understand it myself. I was just surviving, moving forward, but the anger and sadness I couldn't control seeped out in harsh words and painful arguments.

All I recall is me yelling at him to spend more time with me. It would be impossible for him to take a vacation at that point in his career. I remember saying very cruel words like, "You don't love me!" There were more emotionally destructive words that I stabbed his heart with, too. He was begging me to stop arguing and overreacting so much.

Only three months after returning home from the war, I decided unilaterally to move out of our sweet little rented apartment home, to live on the military base. I knew I couldn't control this new sadness, desperation, or rage. My military counselor was sweet, but she offered no diagnosis or helpful suggestions. That marriage ended.

There were broken hearts and shattered dreams all around...

It wasn't until 26 years later, in 2017, while participating in a trauma care course at my local church, that I realized what had happened to me in 1990–

91. There was a name for what I'd been feeling all these years: PTSD. Post-traumatic stress disorder is why I had "dissociated" in the car listening to my tapes from the war. I could have been the poster child for it.

## IF YOU WANT TO ENSURE THAT A PERSON GETS PTSD:

1.  Let them lose a significant loved one to unexpected death.

2.  Quickly isolate them into an active war zone where they must now fight to stay alive.

3.  Suppress all possibilities of them going on their natural grief-healing path.

4.  Give them NO psychological/emotional education, training, or support!

Voila! Nicely set up for PTSD.

The fragments of my life—my grief for my father, my war memories, and the isolation I'd felt. It all pieced together, finally creating a clearer picture of my wounds. The truth emerged, and I could finally see that the young woman I'd been—the newlywed, the daughter grieving her father—had been abandoned.

Another trauma in 2019 pulled me back toward those memories from 1991, and I realized I couldn't go through it alone again. I fearfully reached out to a veteran's center and shared how I was feeling. This time I knew I wasn't suicidal, but somehow feeling familiar darkness that I didn't want to go anywhere near. Been there, done that. No thanks! Stop!

Divine intervention brought me a kind and gentle counselor who knew about PTSD. Keep in mind, it didn't exist much in 1991 yet. For the first time, I found someone who truly listened, who saw all of me, and who agreed with my self-diagnosis.

She listened so softly and tenderly, as I read her my old journal from the war. She heard the sorrow, the fear, and the rage that had built up over decades.

I was finally getting help. Slowly, we worked through my memories, and in time, I was able to forgive myself for leaving parts of me behind. I even enlisted the help of my wartime husband. The PTSD had blocked out most of the actual memories of isolation, exile, and severe longing for my loving family, friends, and civilian life.

Around this time, I became dual-certified as a life and health coach through the Health Coach Institute and took a deep dive into psychology courses on NICABM. I also found Hearts Returning Home, a powerful scripture-based trauma course. I've learned so many excellent tools to transform PTSD into PTS*Growth*.

I've taken the time to go back to my activated soldier in 1991 to show her compassion and educate her on why she was feeling so helpless. The basic definition of trauma is the feeling of helplessness and timelessness, without the adequate resources to become safe again.

In January 2020, my counselor asked, "Why does your 27-year-old soldier still refuse to come out of the arid desert sands?" Her question struck a chord deep within me. I realized that she was waiting for her husband to come and bring her home. But that chapter was closed. My husband had moved on. I had moved on. And yet, a part of me was still waiting.

So, I wrote her a letter.

## MY WISE HEALING SELF THEN WROTE TO THE YOUNG SOLDIER THESE WORDS:

"Dear Captain Wu, MD:

I am so sorry I left you here, all alone in the tan-colored sand dunes of the desert for 30 years. I didn't know you were still waiting.

Please forgive me.

Since the minute I discovered this truth, I have been working so hard to heal and to bring you home.

Thirty years have gone by for the rest of us. I know you're still waiting for your husband, but he has moved on. I have also moved on. Please forgive us, we didn't know.

Would you please come home with me now?

I need your strength now, your innocence, your hope. Our family is going through a tough season, and I need every part of me. Will you finally return home with me, now?"

She agreed. Finally, she agreed. I welcomed her back, the girl on the left who had been left so long ago. She finally left her desert exile.

I was even able to now see how God had hand-picked me to be in the front line, to co-create a new formation with the 5th MASH (FST) (Mobile Army Surgical Hospital (Forward Surgical Team)). The Lord is the Healer and the Restorer.

In my trauma-healing journey, I connected with most of my younger self at various ages and stages. Each letter I wrote to my past self was a bridge, connecting current wisdom and compassion with my younger self's experiences and struggles.

I acknowledged and accepted all that she had been through.

I told her that her sacrifices mattered, that her strength was recognized, and that her pain was not in vain.

I asked her to forgive me for the years I had unknowingly abandoned her, in order to survive the days.

I have visited all ages and parts of ME. My five-year-old baby doll has a pretty cool call-to-life-purpose story. Enough to fill another book. My girls on the left now include: my prenatal embryo, birth, preschooler, teenager, older adult, and parent. Not to mention whatever future stages and seasons there are to grow and evolve through.

Through these healing letters, all versions of me started to re-emerge from the shadows and into the bright, warm, friendly sunlight. Now, I can fully process and recognize her loyalty, her overcoming spirit, and her willingness to sacrifice for those she loved most. These qualities, once hidden beneath layers of survival instincts, began to surface again as I worked diligently to honor, digest, and assimilate them.

I will never abandon or leave behind any part of myself again.

We all have our own guiding forces and influences. My spiritual resources and grounded foundations are through the Creator God. Even though no human being could accompany me during my exile, I was always safe in my heavenly Father's mighty and loving hands.

These verses from Deuteronomy became my lifeline, grounding me during the most challenging parts of my healing journey. I found myself returning to them over and over, allowing each word to sink deep into my soul, reassuring me that I was not alone. It felt as though I was being gently guided all along, even in those moments when I felt abandoned, drifting in an emotional desert.

"The Lord Himself goes before you and will be with you; He will never leave you nor forsake you. Do not be afraid; do not be discouraged."

*Deuteronomy 31:8 NIV*

"Do not be afraid or discouraged, for the Lord will personally go ahead of you. He will be with you; HE will neither fail you nor abandon you."

*Deuteronomy 31:8 NLT*

"Then Moses summoned Joshua. He said to him with all Israel watching, 'Be strong. Take courage. God is striding ahead of you. He's right there with you. He won't let you down; He won't leave you. Don't be intimidated. Don't worry.'"

*Deuteronomy 31:7-8 MSG*

Today, I know that trauma has many faces and many stories. I've learned that the wounds of PTSD cannot be healed in isolation, nor can we simply leave our past selves behind. I've journeyed through myself with curiosity, compassion, and hard-earned wisdom. I've demonstrated to them that a continuing healing journey is possible. We are forever transformed.

I AM now the trauma-refined physician and coach that I desperately needed in 1991.

When I look back, I don't just see a girl on the left, a younger me waiting in the desert.

I see a warrior who endured the unimaginable and found her way home, even when the road was filled with hardship. She is not only the girl who was left behind; she is now the girl who has finally returned home, to ME. Truly grateful to finally feel Whole again, stronger and truer than ever.

I AM the ever-transforming CoachDrWu™.

SCAN TO MEET DR. WU

# BRENDA DEL GRANADO

## BODY TRAUMA,

## RECOVERY & SPINAL ENERGETICS

Imagine living a "normal" life to then realize that what you considered normal was unresolved trauma.

In 2017, life looked successful on paper: I had launched a business, worked a stable corporate job, we were preparing to buy a house, and for the first time, I felt financially free. But then, I started experiencing recurring headaches.

Unfortunately, I was not a stranger to headaches or migraines, as I had dealt with them in high school. But this time felt different; they were persistent, lingering for days, sometimes over a week. As a busy entrepreneur, mom, and wife, I ignored the signs my body was showing me. My hands would tremble, I would sometimes drop things unexpectedly, I felt extremely fatigued, and my brain was in a fog.

This continued for months. Finally, in 2018, my body had enough. I began experiencing severe shooting pains in my head and would visit the ER regularly. I was put on several prescription drugs to alleviate my symptoms, but nothing brought relief.

Eventually, this led to psychogenic seizures, hearing loss in my left ear, and loss of peripheral vision in both eyes. I was a shell of myself, unable to function, let alone be present as a mom or a wife. I was completely debilitated, feeling like I was watching my life slip away. The doctors and specialists seemed at a loss, unable to tell me what was happening. I changed neurologists three times before finally hearing the words:

"You should accept that this is your new normal."

This ushered in one of the darkest periods of my adult life. By 2021, I had been to the hospital over 100 times, endured spinal taps, and seen countless specialists, with little relief in sight. I was exhausted, depressed, and utterly fed up.

In an effort to find answers, I turned to Facebook support groups and online forums for people suffering from undiagnosed chronic pain. I was searching for others who may be experiencing the same symptoms, and most importantly, I was searching for hope. Instead, what I found was more desperation. Lost time and no hope at all. What I found was a community trapped in their suffering.

This was devastating. The hopelessness was overwhelming, and I knew I couldn't let myself become one of them. I was at my wit's end. It was either find a solution or completely give up, and I was not a quitter. It became clear to me that I would never accept this as my new reality. I couldn't. I wanted to live and thrive. I wanted to wake up pain-free, enjoy my children, and get back to my life, plus the future I still believed in.

Determined to reclaim my life, I sought out alternative medicine and delved into research about undiagnosed pain and holistic practices. This is where I found a glimmer of hope.

My name is Brenda Del Granado, I am 37 years old. I am a mother to two amazing children and the owner of Two Moons Studio in the DC Metropolitan Area. Today, I am a Spinal Energetics and Reiki Practitioner, with an unwavering passion for deep healing and self-love advocacy.

I dedicate my life to helping individuals regulate their nervous systems, reconnect with their bodies, and unlock their potential through alternative healing methods. The person I am today was because of the experiences, challenges, and battles I faced and conquered.

This is the story of how chronic pain led me to the opportunity for profound healing. As aforementioned, I was desperate for relief. So much so that I flew over three thousand miles to the country of El Salvador, to see a naturopathic doctor. I'd love to tell you that through my extensive research, I found this doctor, but the truth is that a friend of my ex-husband found him.

You know that saying what goes around comes around? Well, during the pandemic, this friend, his wife, and his two daughters needed a place to live while transitioning to this country. Our home is small and humble, but our hearts are big, so we offered them a place to stay. I believe, that it is because of this act of kindness that we were referred to the naturopathic doctor. We would have likely not found him if it weren't for this man, and I will forever be grateful to him.

Once in El Salvador, we made our way to his office. We got there at 6 a.m. to wait in a long line with so many other hopeful people who had also traveled far and wide. After hours, we were finally called in, and within three days of working with this doctor, most of my symptoms had subsided. I was prescribed heavy detox tinctures, a strict regimen of Vitamin B complex shots, and very deep physical therapy.

I returned home to the States and continued with the doctor's instructions. After three months, all my symptoms were gone. I was pain-free for the first time in years. I felt whole again. My family was relieved, and for the first time, I felt I could start living again.

It was through the experience of chronic pain that I was able to get down to the nitty-gritty of why and when this physical pain cycle started in the first place. This doctor told me that my chronic pain came from a chronic state of stress (fight or flight). Like a tension headache that never went away, my tense muscles compressing the nerves around my head. Squeezing and causing unbearable pressure. This is very likely caused by my inability to let go of control.

Then came the moment of revelation. I remember it as if it were yesterday. My doctor asked me, "What is the first memory that comes to mind, of a time you felt out of control?" At first, I was confused, but then a memory surfaced—one I had locked away so tightly I didn't even know I had buried it. It was a memory that would hold the key to understanding my pain.

I immediately realized that I had purposefully made myself forget it. A protective mechanism surrounded this memory. I didn't consciously do it, but it was locked away, and the key I didn't even know existed suddenly appeared in my hand. It was months before I decided that not using the key would cause more harm because the only way out was through.

As a teenager, I had low self-esteem and struggled with feelings of self-worth. Years of bullying had left me feeling like the outcast, the "four-eyed fat girl" no one wanted to be friends with. I became angry, resentful, and rebellious. Finally, one day I stood up for myself and started getting into fights. It scared others away from picking on me, but the whole time I was still feeling small. I tried reinventing myself, taking on an alter ego to make getting through school possible.

I sought attention and validation from others, especially from guys, which led me into some questionable situations that weren't always safe. It was my sophomore year of high school, I met a man at the mall while hanging out with my best friend. Little did I know that my need for attention and validation would create the perfect storm of vulnerability. This man later became one of the scariest monsters a nightmare could ever create.

I was raped by this man, who then also forced me to have sexual intercourse with his friends. I was forced to endure things that no teenager should. I was a scared teen who was groomed and manipulated. The shame and disgust I felt were so overwhelming that I never told anyone. I kept it all inside, and this darkness took root in my body and mind.

These events sent me spiraling down a dark path. The darkest a teenager should ever have to experience. Depression, bulimia, and even a suicide attempt followed. I believe that as soon as I experienced this trauma, both my nervous system and heart became stuck in a "fight or flight" response.

I buried my trauma deep, building an impenetrable wall between myself and that younger version of me. I believe that as soon as I experienced this trauma, my body, my nervous system, and my heart got stuck in a state of chronic fight or flight. It was an entire rebellion, vowing to never be out of control ever again.

For years, I carried the weight of these repressed memories. Locking away the trauma and building an impenetrable wall between myself and my body, protecting yet also trapping that young girl inside. Completely disassociating. Never able to connect intimately with myself or my future partners. Always ignoring its needs and wants. Giving, helping, and fixing for everyone except myself.

The need to control everything around me became paramount, but in my pursuit of control, I disconnected from the one thing that needed the most healing—myself. I became an over-achiever, burying myself in work and goals. I used every excuse in the book; I'm not a quitter, I need to finish this, I will rest when I'm dead, no one will care more about my business than me, I can do it all... etc.

I was on the burnout cycle, always chasing the next business idea and "success." I was an entrepreneur, and that was the territory, the characteristics that came with that title. Anything to keep me busy, my mind preoccupied, and my body on the go.

Over time, this disconnection manifested as chronic physical pain, often undiagnosed and misunderstood by doctors. I began to uncover memories I'd hidden, and in facing them, I finally understood how deeply my trauma had affected my body and mind. The healing journey wasn't easy, but it was necessary.

I faced my trauma, embraced the younger me, and began to forgive—not only others but myself.

In that healing space, I realized that the pain I had carried for so long was not just physical but emotional, mental, and deeply tied to the trauma I had disassociated from for years. I realized that every tension in my body held a story I hadn't dared to confront. My muscles, constantly clenched, were guarding wounds I had forced myself to forget.

Each time I closed my eyes, old memories began to surface, showing me that the pain had always been a message—a plea from my body to be acknowledged and healed. The physical walls were just a reflection of the walls around my heart and mind. My nervous system was shot. All it knew how to do was bury itself in work, stay busy, never settle down, unable to be calm or be at peace.

Through alternative practices, like breath work, meditation, Reiki, and Spinal Energetics, I was able to reconnect with my body in ways I never thought possible. I learned new methods to maintain that connection, allowing me to move through the pain, rather than remain imprisoned by it. The journey wasn't easy, but it was necessary. Facing the trauma, loving the parts of me that put myself in these situations, and accepting the parts I played in these experiences. Looking inward and healing from within.

Talking to my inner child/teenager, embracing little Brenda, and holding space for her while she let go of the trauma. Reassuring her that she is still worthy and loved even with the experience she has lived through. Facing my deep mother and father wounds that surrounded that time of my life and forgiving not only others but myself. Allowing the shame, anger, and sadness to come through versus repressing them. I had to grieve that part of me that was taken and mourn the loss of who I was so that I could become who I am. Through the darkness, I found the light.

Talking about it was never an option for me. I swallowed all the words, every single one that I ever wanted to express, every single time I repressed them. After digging deeper, doing the work to heal, and letting go, I realized that what made me sick was the silence. It took me a while to be able to talk about it.

I started by writing everything down. Then, I decided to tell my mother what had happened to me. I never wanted her to know, I wanted to protect her from pain, but because I had worked through this, I was able to. I was also able to be there for her as she now experienced the emotions that come from learning that something like this happened to her child.

I knew that talking about it would help not only me but others as well. Eventually, I even told my daughter and my son. I did this to make them aware of the dangerous situations we can often put ourselves in. Explained the need I felt to always be validated by others and where I was in my life when this happened to me.

These difficult conversations provided many opportunities for my children to learn more about this world, their mother, and themselves. Allowing them the gift of knowledge and a safe space to ask questions.

Learning to let go of control wasn't easy.

It felt like giving up a part of my identity. I'd spent years managing not only my own challenges but also trying to shoulder the struggles of others around me. Releasing that grip meant facing the fear that maybe, without control, everything could fall apart. But as I allowed myself to surrender, I realized the opposite was true.

My vulnerability became my strength, and letting go felt like finally setting down a heavy burden I'd carried alone for far too long. Each step toward release felt like reclaiming a small piece of myself.

Today, I can finally say that my trauma no longer defines me. I have reclaimed my life, and my mission is to help others who are suffering in silence as I once did. Those suppressing memories they may likely not even recall because they, too, are protecting themselves. Too many people carry the weight of invisible chains. But if my story can offer them a glimmer of hope, I will share it.

I've come to realize that my story, sadly, isn't as unique as I once thought. Many have experienced similar traumas, traumas that are often locked away, not spoken about, and left to fester in silence. Too many people continue to live with those invisible chains, never truly moving through the pain. I've learned that the only way out is through.

We must face those dark places to heal and our body tells the story.

We just need to listen to it.

If I were to pinpoint what makes my story unique, it would be my resilience. I refused to accept that my life would always be defined by pain. I went to extreme lengths to reclaim my health and my sense of self, even traveling across the world for answers when none could be found closer to home. Now, I am called to share my story because I want others to know that they, too, can reclaim not only their life but their power.

Choosing myself wasn't just about managing pain—it was about redefining what it meant to live fully. This choice shifted everything: the way I approached my work, my relationships, and even the smallest daily decisions.

I began surrounding myself with people and environments that nurtured my spirit. I set new boundaries, choosing joy, health, and authenticity over the old patterns of self-sacrifice. This transformation was a reminder that my worth wasn't tied to enduring suffering, but to embracing the life I truly wanted to create.

Choosing myself after all that I've been through has become my greatest achievement. If I can choose myself after all that I've been through, I hope to inspire others to do the same. This anthology is about self-worth, and I want to contribute my voice to remind every reader that they are worthy of healing, worthy of being chosen, and, most importantly, worthy of choosing themselves.

With love,
Brenda

SCAN TO MEET BRENDA

# DIANE JACOBS NATOLI
## MARRIAGE, LOSS & SELF-WORTH

My name is Diane Jacobs Natoli. I'm a wife, a mom, and a certified life and health coach. And if you'd told me 30 years ago that I'd be any of those things, especially the last one, I probably would've laughed. Life has a funny way of throwing us into roles we never saw coming.

Let's go back to 1993, the year I first got married. I was about 250 pounds, but I wasn't sitting around thinking about my weight all the time. I was happy, I loved my life, but yeah, I knew I could be healthier. So, by December of the following year, my husband and I decided to make a change. We'd had enough of feeling sluggish and just wanted to see if we could feel a little better day to day. We started small—eating better, going for walks, simple stuff. And honestly? I was feeling pretty good. I felt like, okay, maybe this health kick could be something we stick to.

Then, just a few weeks later, in January 1995, everything changed. I was diagnosed with multiple sclerosis. That was a wake-up call like nothing I'd ever experienced. Multiple sclerosis is no joke; it hits everyone differently, and for me, it was rough from the start. My walking got shaky, I'd lose my balance, and my vision would blur at the worst times. The whole world around me was out of focus, and so was my future. The fear? It was almost paralyzing.

At the time, I was working as an office manager and surgical assistant for a plastic surgeon. I loved that job, and I was stubbornly determined to keep it. My boss, bless him, went out of his way to help me. He'd set me up with IV steroid treatments right in the office when I needed them. Those steroids didn't fix things, but they helped me get by day to day.

The first few months after my diagnosis were brutal. I'd lie in bed at night, my mind racing with all these "what-ifs." I kept thinking, *Is this it?* Am I just supposed to accept that this is my life now? There was this anger, this frustration at feeling like my body had betrayed me. But I knew, deep down, that I had two options: I could give in and let the MS run my life, or I could get up and figure out how to live with it.

Slowly but surely, I chose the second option. I decided that I wasn't just going to sit around waiting for life to pass me by. I started thinking about all the people out there struggling in their own ways, people who needed someone to remind them they could still live a damn good life, no matter what they were going through. That's when I started thinking about becoming a coach. I wanted to take what I'd learned and use it to help others see their own strength, especially on the days when they didn't feel it themselves.

Today, that's what I do. I work with people who feel stuck, who need someone to tell them the truth straight, but also to remind them that they can still write their own stories. It doesn't matter what you weigh, what illness you're dealing with, or what your life looks like right now. What matters is how you show up for yourself. If you can do that, you're already stronger than you think.

So, yeah, MS was a curveball I never expected. But if it's taught me anything, it's that I can handle more than I ever thought possible—and so can you.

Surprisingly, at the age of 22, I still hadn't started my menstrual cycle. The doctors always told me that it was near impossible for me to have children, and at the time, I believed them. For most of my life, it felt like my body was working against me. But then something miraculous happened. The medication I was taking for my MS triggered my period for the first time, and in March of 1996, I found out I was pregnant. I could hardly believe it—after years of being told I couldn't have children, there I was, carrying a life inside me. My amazing son was born in January 1997.

However, motherhood wasn't the only challenge I was facing. Due to my poor eyesight, I was forced to leave my job. It was a tough decision, but I knew it was the right one. Losing my career added to the stress, but I wasn't ready to give up on life just yet. My husband and I continued on our weight loss journey, and I eventually lost 120 pounds. It felt like a personal victory, but it wasn't enough to save my marriage. My husband and I began to drift apart. I didn't feel loved or appreciated, and eventually, I stepped out of our marriage. I met a man, and for a time, he filled the emotional void I'd been carrying. This man became my second husband. Our marriage lasted five years, but over time, it became clear that it wasn't meant to last.

In 2015, I met someone else. I fell madly in love with him. It felt like a new chapter in my life, one where I could finally experience the joy I'd been longing for. We were happy. For a while, everything felt right. But as time went on, I began to see cracks in the facade. He was an alcoholic. The man I loved became someone I barely recognized. I was verbally and mentally abused. I was gaslighted on a daily basis. I became fearful, broken, and filled with self-doubt. The woman I was before felt like a distant memory.

Even though things were falling apart, I didn't want to give up. He eventually went to rehab, and for a time, things got better. We even got married. But in 2017, the cycle repeated itself. He relapsed. I didn't know how much more I could take, but I stayed, thinking that things would get better, just like before. I had no idea how wrong I was.

Then, on October 20, 2017, my worst fear came true. I came home to find him dead on the bathroom floor. He had passed away from his addiction. My world came crashing down. Everything I thought I knew was shattered in an instant. The man I had loved, the man I had tried to save, was gone. I was left alone, scared, and heartbroken. My life, once filled with hope and possibility, had been reduced to grief and confusion.

That moment marked a turning point in my life. I had to face the fact that I couldn't keep living in the shadows of others' decisions. I had to find a way out of the darkness. It wasn't easy, and it didn't happen overnight, but I began to rebuild. I had to rediscover myself—the woman who had lost so much but was still standing. I had to reclaim my strength and my worth, even when everything felt impossible.

Since that day, I've learned that healing doesn't come from avoiding pain but from facing it head-on. I've had to forgive myself, which was one of the hardest things I've ever done. I've had to let go of guilt, shame, and fear. I've had to find peace within myself, and only then could I truly move forward.

For six weeks after my husband's passing, I was a wreck. I was hysterically crying, completely lost in my grief. I was screaming at my now deceased husband, pleading for him to send me someone who would love me for me, someone who wouldn't try to change me. I felt so broken, so desperate for connection. I wanted to feel seen, to feel like I mattered again. I just didn't know how I could move forward. That night, through my tears and despair, I went online, just searching for anything: any distraction, anything that might bring me peace. As I scrolled aimlessly, my eyes locked on a photo of a man. A friendly face. A man who lived in New Jersey, which seemed like a lifetime away from my home in Long Island. Still, something about that picture drew me in. Maybe it was the warmth in his eyes, maybe it was the feeling that there was still something out there for me.

I messaged him, not knowing what would come of it. And to my surprise, he replied. Ronnie, that man from New Jersey, came to meet me just two days later. We hit it off immediately. I don't know how to explain it, but it felt like a light was shining again. I wasn't alone in the world anymore. We kept seeing each other regularly, and after a while, I made the decision to move to New Jersey to be with him. It felt like the beginning of something new. For the first time in years, I wasn't just surviving—I was starting to feel alive again.

But just as life was starting to look up, my world was rocked again. In 2019, my mom, who had always been my biggest cheerleader, my best friend, and my rock, got sick. I had always gone to her for advice, and she was the one who told me time and time again, "When are you going to hang out your shingle? Everyone comes to you for help and advice. You've got the skills, the knowledge, and the heart. Why aren't you doing this for yourself?"

I looked at her, and I felt so lost. I was disabled. My vision was poor, my hands didn't allow me to write legibly, and I had a constant fear of falling. Who would ever hire me? How could I even help others when I was struggling with so many of my own limitations? I was allowing my disabilities to define my abilities, and I couldn't see beyond that.

My mom passed away in September of 2019, and with her, I lost a part of myself. I thought the grief would swallow me whole. I felt paralyzed, not just by the pain of losing her but by the weight of everything I had yet to accomplish. But it was in that moment of loss that something inside me shifted. I had to ask myself, "What would she want me to do?"

It was then that I saw an advertisement on Facebook for Health Coach Institute, offering a dual life and health coaching certification program. Could I really do this? Could I overcome my fears and limitations and finally take that step toward helping others, just like my mom had always encouraged me to do? After talking it through with Ronnie, we both agreed—I could do this. I could build something for myself, despite all the obstacles I faced.

So, I dove in. I poured my heart and soul into those nine months of training. It wasn't easy. I struggled with my health, my disabilities, and my own doubts, but I refused to quit. I pushed through it all, day by day, and on the other side of it, I stood with my dual certification in hand. I had done it. I had achieved something I never thought was possible.

Now, I am living my dream. Every day, I wake up excited to help my clients find their own paths to healing and happiness. They tell me that I've saved their lives. They say that I listened when no one else did, that I validated their feelings and helped them navigate their pain. For me, there's no greater reward than hearing that I made a difference in someone's life. I've learned that sometimes, all people need is to feel heard, to know that they aren't alone in their struggles. That's what I strive to give my clients—the understanding and support that I didn't always have when I was at my lowest.

I've always believed that when we lead with generosity, it tends to come back to us, one way or another. Karma works both ways, and I've found that if you put good energy out there, it somehow circles back. That's why I offer a lot of my work pro bono—because it feels like the right thing to do. And honestly, even if it doesn't come back in the way you expect, there's a personal fulfillment that comes with just being there for others. It helps me keep my own craft sharp, too. You know, like keeping your bike-riding skills fresh, or getting back into the car after a while. It's important to keep practicing, to stay vibrant and connected to the work that drives me.

Around 2021, I was in a ShopRite, talking to my boyfriend at the time when my phone rang. It was a mom looking for life coaching for her daughter. She asked why I wasn't guaranteeing my services. I remember saying, "I don't know your daughter." How can I guarantee anything? I can promise that I'll show up, that I'll do my best, but I can't guarantee her results. If someone's not willing to do their part, what's the point? So, I told her, I was not promising something that was out of my control. I can't guarantee her success—only that I'll be there every step of the way.

I have to laugh because that conversation led to one of the most meaningful relationships in my life. After three months of coaching, this woman called me, all worked up about needing a job. We hadn't even touched on what she did for a living! Turns out, she was an experienced bookkeeper and did computer work, which led me to offer her a chance to work with my boyfriend, who was looking for someone to handle his books. She's been with us ever since, and I truly consider her one of my best friends now. Her mom still calls me, saying, "You saved my daughter's life," and I tell you, that's the most rewarding thing I can imagine.

When it comes to the women I work with—especially wives of alcoholics—I see a lot of common pain points. They're often gaslighted, financially abused, and stripped of their self-worth. It's not just the drinking; it's the constant manipulation. I've seen it time and time again—these women are given a tiny allowance, just enough to take care of their children, and they're left mentally crippled. They don't believe they deserve love or appreciation. They've been made to feel like they're the problem, when really, the only thing they're doing wrong is disrespecting themselves.

I always say, "You don't have to leave. If you choose to stay, that's your choice. But let's focus on *you* first. We're not going to fix the marriage. Let's work on your sense of self." Some of them have left, and it's been life-changing. One woman, for example, now lives in her own place. It's small, but it's *hers*. Everything in it is hers, and she's stronger for it. That's the goal. To feel empowered and know that you can create your own life, regardless of your circumstances.

As I reflect on my journey, I realize that all the struggles and heartaches, all the failures and setbacks, were the very things that made me who I am today. I've learned more from my pain than I ever could have from my successes. And for that, I am deeply grateful. I wouldn't change a thing. The lessons I've learned along the way have shaped me into the woman I am now—a woman who has found her strength, her purpose, and her passion.

There's power in realizing that no one is perfect and that you're not a failure for making mistakes. There's a lot of judgment that can come with being married and divorced multiple times. I posted about this recently online, and someone commented, asking if I hadn't seen the red flags before in my previous marriages. I told them, "I didn't post this for you to judge me. But if you want to judge, go ahead. I know who I am, and my current husband knows who I am. That's all that matters."

Life doesn't have to end because of mistakes or situations. You can get out of any mess you're in. And while there are extreme cases where it takes intervention, most of the time, it's about changing your mindset and your self-talk. Stop beating yourself up for what you allowed to happen, and just don't let it happen again.

But, you know, in marriage, as the years go on, you'll realize that not everything has to be said. You might want to tell your husband to shut up, or that he's kidding, but there's a way to say things. You'll always have normal annoyances from daily life. Like, when he says, "Feel like making me dinner?" I'll be like, "No, not really," but I'll cook because I know we should eat.

But in terms of cooking, I don't trust him in my kitchen. He makes a mess, and I clean as I go. I don't want to deal with a disaster. Stay out of my kitchen and my laundry!

My biggest piece of advice? Lean on someone. Don't fight your battles alone. In today's world, there's always someone out there who gets it. There's a support system, even if it doesn't always feel like it. Reach out to someone. Find your tribe, your people.

In April 2024, Ronnie and I married. After everything I've been through, I finally feel like I am living the life of my dreams. The woman who once felt broken, lost, and alone is now standing strong, surrounded by love and purpose. The journey wasn't easy, but I wouldn't have it any other way. I've learned that the most beautiful parts of life often come from the most difficult moments, and I'm finally ready to embrace whatever comes next with open arms.

When I think back to moments that changed me, I think it was when my previous husband passed away from alcoholism. Something shifted in me, I became stronger, and I realized my worth. That was when I had to step up. I never had a clear image of what marriage or a husband should be, so I was flying blind for a long time. I wanted things to work, but I couldn't fix everything. And when he passed, I had to figure everything out on my own, from the house we bought to the bills. I did it.

Even though I have been through a lot, I truly feel it was all done *for* me, not *to* me.

I'm not just surviving anymore—I'm thriving. And that, to me, is a victory in itself.

SCAN TO MEET DIANE

# TIFFANY O'HEARN

## ABUSE, ALCHEMY & SPIRITUALITY

We were in a dark room, with the only light coming from the monitors, the cacophony of peeping signaling life and death with only a lapse in the tones. The usual hospital smells permeate through me, sterile, sick, and dying, as I stare down at my father. He is a strong, brave, resilient, kind, loving, man shrouded in blankets as his brain tumor grows and ravages the handsome being beneath.

My brother is there with me. I am sitting on the edge of the bed, my brother is perched by his head. We all are so intimately aware of the life being drained beneath. You can see and feel the pain in my dad's eyes for being the impatience to our distress, and also the peace and love within that this experience provides us along our journey.

Often there are moments in our lives that live with us. That speaks through us, and cannot be forgotten. They hold feelings, emotions, and knowing within them. You know, in those times, they are the pinnacle of your journey, your story, and your inner evolution. The choice lies within us to see it in and with love, and experience it, no matter the pain it feels in the moment, for the memory is funny like that. When we think back, we remember with less pain and more love. This has at least been my experience.

I am 28 years old, my brother is a few weeks shy of 27. Our father is 47. There are not many years between the ages, only experience and the wear of a difficult life exist between us all. Dad is speaking from the heart. You can feel the love surrounding us, the tears, the wounds, the intertwined lives of the three of us. You could feel the heart growing between us all. Knowing at the time that this intimate special moment was numbered. My human experience is wrought with pain and despair, my spiritual body is embracing the beautiful lessons I've yet to experience. His message to me fourteen years later only now makes sense to me. His words don't have the confusion they once held, the wonder to know if I was doing it "right," for now I know.

Ever since I can remember, which now I am realizing goes beyond what I can recall consciously, I had this inner knowing. A knowing that life isn't exactly as it seems. I would be in the presence of adults and feel their wounds, their pain all around me. I felt it. I have unknowingly, in my young mind, been a student to humans. Adults were abundant around me, and my family unit would demand that these adults be held up on a pedestal, for they are adults. I knew that life was not as it seemed, not as they told me it was. I could see and feel differently. Naturally, having a big curious mind about humans and behaviors invited the feelings of being unseen, unwitnessed, and misunderstood. I assumed my job, at a very young age, was to fix them, please them, and show them the divinity within.

I was about three years old, and I was sitting on the floor in our apartment. I was crying. I could feel and see my mom in distress, in my young mind, my cries were in an effort to divert her attention from the growing frustration. My cries went unanswered. On the floor, crying, my young mind decided I needed to try harder. This was on repeat throughout my childhood and my life. I see and feel my mom in pain, and I find ways to ease it or take it away. It wasn't often received (and it's not my mom's fault). These experiences of pleasing and fixing continuously caused me these tiny traumas of the heart, while the feelings of being unseen and misunderstood became a second language.

I was born an empath, a sensitive child who would witness the world and feel it all. Oftentimes, it was dramatic the effects it would have on me. In my young mind, if I could see the pain, I could fix the pain, save them from themselves, or at least distract them enough. And I did. My empathy trumped my boundaries, my compassion stripped me of my autonomy, and all the while, people still hurt all around me. The truth of it was, deep down, my pain was as well. A well of wounds seeping through the earth, collecting sadness, fear, anger, and hurt within my roots.

My childhood showed me many things. Lessons I took with me, and still do. It was not an easy one, and that is okay, for I know within my own wounds are stories, lessons, and love. This is the cornerstone of who I am today: love. And that was the message I received in the dark room all those years ago. My father, after speaking to my brother, tears are pouring down our faces, in love, pain, and promises. He looked at me with so much love and adoration, his hand still held the power within as we clasped them around each other. I remember after he shared with me, thinking, *Huh, he gave my brother so much more.* He did not. He gave us what we needed to hear. It was as if his spirit body was sharing these messages with us. He looked at me and said, "Tiff, find love. Find love."

I recall the simplicity of the message, and the desire within me to achieve the wish he bestowed on me. I can do that. I can find love.

My father lasted another month after that night. The loss of him cut me open, it seemed. It changed me in such a deep way that words cannot express. During the last few months of his illness, I had befriended a woman. She would check up on me, especially the last ten days we spent in hospice with him. In feeling into this request of his, I allowed the friendship to grow. In my pain and wounds, there was a person who was there, LOVE! There it is. The problem in reflection was the love that I thought I was asked to find took me further away from myself. The intuition I had seemed distant and quiet. The human underneath was separating from the spirit from the wholeness within. I dove head first into a toxic and very abusive relationship that started as friends and ended in heartbreak.

Two months before my father's diagnosis of a brain tumor, he helped me move into the new home I purchased. A place that was mine, it was safe, it was all I could have asked for—it was home. I was fortunate enough to have a huge walk-in closet. Shortly after we had started dating, she proposed to me. I had walked into my closet, and there on the dresser behind the door was a ring with a note, "Will you marry me?" I was stuck. My spirit was beckoning me to deny this request, my ego was telling me, *You can't say no.* So, I walked out of the closet and pretended as if I had not seen it. We had an event we were headed to and ignored the very large elephant between us. I was twisted up inside. Ultimately knowing I was going to say yes. We returned home, and she asked me the question. I said yes because I was going to please her, fix her, and save her from herself. The seven years together were a difficult time, and the journey within was necessary and needed to know what I know now, and I am grateful.

Our relationship was not good, and our marriage was not great, but the child I had within was a gift, a gift I so openly received. She was two when we split ways. I was alone. I had only begun to unwrap the last 7 years, but really the last 36 years. I had not consciously realized how isolated I was, how the wounds of pleasing and fixing had me in this experience that felt so terrible in the moment, but it also held so much opportunity. What was born was this deep desire within to figure out who I was, who that person was that showed up in that marriage in that relationship, and to redefine ME. And, I did.

My relationship with my daughter (she is now 8) was one I bore with total intention. Intention as to the parent I would be for her, I took all the good I had witnessed, and the bad I experienced and intentionally vowed to be different. To not be a parent simply because I was pregnant, to choose to be a mom from my spirit rather than my ego. I did that, mostly, because I could only give as much as I had. Without that love within, the love outside of ourselves will follow along the boundaries we have created. Love is pure, non-conditional, and the most beautiful thing we get to experience.

I am not the girl I once was, I am not the woman I once was. And, I should not be. We are all on a journey, and we cannot have had today without yesterday. Yesterday I knew something different, today, I know more. This is life, and how it goes. We only need to be intentional within it, feel it, honor it, and move through it. As I shed these old layers of myself, I do so with love and compassion, for I am me. The wounds and the lessons have been the most paramount in my journey, and I look back at her with love and adoration.

After my divorce, and many years later, I felt I was chasing this love. Looking for it. Being a mom brought forth love, a love that I have not experienced, a love pure and unconditional. A love that invites me to continue down this path of healing, for me, her, and humanity. She may be my greatest teacher in love.

It is easy to give love, to share in this vibration, the divinity; however, it begs the question of intention. So much of my journey has been at the helm of love. From looking for it to feeling it and, more importantly, being it. Through these steps along the way, I have come to define that love, that love that I had been seeking.

About two years ago, I was feeling self-love. In this meditation, you visualize a tree. The roots are our roots, they are beneath, plentiful, and hidden. We see the trunk, and within this trunk is the love we have for ourselves. The branches are the love we have outside of ourselves, or for others. I saw my tree. It was on the brink of toppling over. How could that be? I love so many people. What I learned is that our trunk is directly correlated with the love we have for ourselves and the love we have for others. So much of my life I have been programmed to have more branches than trunk. I feel the same is true for you.

It feels damn good to love, but I found that the love outside of myself drowned out the love I had for myself. My love would topple over if I didn't work on myself, work on my roots. The root of why I have dismissed myself, my wants, needs, and autonomy, and given it all away. Keeping only the parts that allow me to survive. In feeling into the message to find love, it started to make sense. Perhaps the request was to find love within.

Like any event in our life, lessons, and learnings, often take time to root, to manifest wholly within our life. This takes time because, again, we cannot take it all in at once. It is a process, a growth. This summer, I was called to evaluate my life: to reflect, to witness, and to hold with love.

These wounds I held throughout my life were dissolving with my energy-healing practices. I was seeing the side of myself I always knew existed. One that was more able to respond lovingly to life, to connect with my intuition as the governing voice, not my ego. I was seeing myself in all areas, being intentional, for we cannot change anything without intention. Intention allows us to see, it calls for us to witness without judgment, and when we do, then, and only then, can we shift. I was being called to shift. I had made great progress on my internal tree trunk, but I was still missing something.

I was feeling out of alignment with the love I had to the love I was able to receive. The harmony between the two was not balanced. So, I hit the trails. I spent six nights in the woods with my partner, under the stars, being intentional with what I was seeking. I entered the woods with clear intentions, I knew Mother Gia held the answers, and she did.

Again, I was brought to my knees. Her wisdom showed me that being out of alignment was our greatest opportunity to find that connection to the divine love within. I was not loving in alignment with love because I was missing so much within. I had let my love for myself float away into many yeses, to promises I knew I shouldn't have made, to silencing my voice for the pleasure of others.

Nature is love. If you truly witness nature, you see harmony and rhythm. It has an essence and a vibration that is unmatched. Nature, under any conditions, thrives. I could see this and feel this with every fiber of my being. I remember sitting in the dirt, eating my lunch on my backpacking trip. I was happily resting and nourishing my body for the later part of the hike, then I looked down and there were ants all around me. They were unaffected by my presence. They were doing what they needed to do to live. To thrive. I looked to my left, and there were more insects, traveling about, going around me, again unafflicted by my presence. I paused. These tiny beings create this immense understanding. The understanding that we are all important, we are all God's creations—nature is love, and we are nature. I was cultivating this gently into my life.

My father's voice echoed in the woods as nature amplified this whisper. I was giving so much of myself away, unintentionally and inappropriately. Love doesn't nurture resentment. Love doesn't foster stress. Love is amplified by our truths, by standing rooted in our values, and in integrity for ourselves. My father exists in a place of only pure, unconditional love, and how can I bring this to my human self? For my spirit knows love, so does yours. Without intention, we can not root it into the physical realm.

This summer was poignant and dramatic. What I learned was that to be devoted to self is to be devoted to love. So, I became that. Devoted to healing my wounds, transforming my programs, and releasing my past life traumas with love and humility. These wounds of pleasing others are being stripped away, for I don't need them anymore. I need me, I need love.

I am still a student of love, a student of me. But, I know now that message delivered to me 14 years ago was never about finding love outside of myself. It was a message to step into me. To find that sacred love within, nurture it, and continue to cultivate it through experiences. For this is not a time when love is not present. Love is in what I do. I have been tested within this, and I know it to be true. We need to devote ourselves to the love within. To ourselves. Take time to fall in love with you. Romance you. Do all the things that bring us closer to self. Journal, dance, meditate, immerse yourself in nature, feel the music, move your body, read, connect to the divine voice within, and nourish your mind, body, and soul intentionally. And heal. To heal our wounds is to rise above and hold yourself in a space and place of love, at all times. For we are loving beings. Connect to your own roots, and grow your trunk. Feel that love you have within and continue to meet it. For Dad was all-knowing all those years ago, feeling death and feeling love.

What I know now is that love is eternal.

**SCAN TO MEET TIFFANY**

# TANIA RIZOSKI

## HUSTLE, HEALING & ALIGNMENT

I was born in Macedonia in 1974, and when I was around 18 months old, my parents made the decision to move back to Australia. They are both Macedonian, and although we lived in a reasonably conservative household with a lot of cultural traditions, the church wasn't a big part of our lives. We were raised with the belief in God, but attending church on a regular basis wasn't something we did.

In Macedonian culture, men are traditionally the breadwinners, while women stay home to raise the family and maintain the household. That was the norm I grew up with, and living in Albion Park Rail, NSW, didn't provide a lot of opportunities at the time. After finishing my HSC, I went straight into a full-time admin job, but I didn't have big career aspirations. What I really wanted was simple: to find a loving husband and have four kids by the time I was 30. That was my dream.

At 21 years and 9 months, I married a wonderful man, and we moved to Sydney. By the age of 27, I had two beautiful children. Although we decided not to have any more kids, I felt like I had achieved my goal. What I didn't realise at the time was that moving to Sydney would open my eyes to so much more than I could have ever imagined.

Growing up in a semi-sheltered lifestyle and being married so young, I hadn't considered the opportunities that existed beyond my small town. Suddenly, a new passion emerged within me:

Working in the corporate world.

Since moving to Sydney, I had always worked full-time. We lived with my in-laws for the first five and a half years of marriage, so I only took nine months off after each of my children was born. I was blessed to have that support around me at the time.

My career journey started in accounts, but I quickly developed an interest in becoming a Personal Assistant, something I had thought about when I was younger but never pursued. Fortunately, the organisation I worked for was large enough to offer opportunities for growth, and over the course of my 10 years there, I transitioned from accounts to be in a Personal Assistant role. I loved it, and this career path led me to become an Executive Assistant, a journey that spanned approximately 17 years.

Still, deep down, I knew there was something more for me, even if I couldn't pinpoint what it was. When I accepted a role at a Non-Profit as the Executive Assistant to the Chief

Executive Officer (CEO), everything started to shift. About a year into the job, a new CEO came on board. He saw something in me, something I hadn't even seen in myself. He believed I was capable of more, and he gave me the opportunity to move into a management role, and later into a General Manager position.

The role and the area of the business I was working in were completely new to me, and honestly, it came out of nowhere. But I recognised it as an opportunity too good to pass up, I had a quote from Richard Branson running in my mind, "If somebody offers you an amazing opportunity but you are not sure you can do it, say yes, then learn how to do it later."

So, I said yes, even though I had no idea how I was going to figure it all out.

During those next seven years, I learned more than I ever expected—not just about leadership, but about myself. I learned the difference between managing people and truly leading them. I navigated office politics at a whole new level and began to understand what kind of leader I wanted to be—and what kind I didn't. It was a period of immense growth, but I realised that I needed more formal education to support my next steps.

So, I made the decision, and it wasn't an easy one, but thankfully, I had the support of my family to pursue an MBA (Master of Business Administration), even though I had never studied at the university level before. The timing was tough—I was 45, juggling a senior leadership role, supporting two kids at home, and helping my husband with his business, but deep down, I knew I needed this degree to step into the next phase of my career. It felt like the ultimate test of my resilience and ability to manage it all, but I was prepared to give it a go.

The first year of the MBA in mid-2019 was challenging but manageable. It was during the pandemic in 2020, however, that things took a turn. Suddenly, the world was upside down, and everything required more energy—working from home, managing the uncertainty, helping my kids navigate remote learning and remote working, and helping to care for my mum, who had been diagnosed with a serious illness in mid-2020.

My mother's illness added a huge emotional weight on me, particularly with the pandemic throwing in its own set of challenges around lockdowns and me being able to travel back and forth from Sydney to Albion Park. I found myself staying up late into the night, burning the candle at both ends to meet deadlines while continuing to perform at work.

But over the course of three years, I did it. I completed my MBA in mid-2022, but not without a cost. Just a few months after completing my degree, I hit a wall. It wasn't a typical kind of exhaustion; this was deeper. My body was screaming for rest in a way I had never experienced before. I couldn't get out of bed without feeling drained. Even thinking felt like an incredibly difficult task. I was diagnosed with adrenal fatigue, something I had never even heard of before, but this was burnout on a level I couldn't have imagined—mentally, emotionally, and physically. I was exhausted and constantly drained.

Looking back, it made perfect sense. I had pushed myself beyond my limits for so long that my body had no choice but to shut down.

It was during this time that I realised I needed to heal, and that's when my spiritual journey began. My spiritual awakening came during this period of forced rest. It began with an unexpected nudge to see a psychic, something

I had always been fearful of. But this time, there was no fear, only excitement and curiosity. That visit sparked something within me, opening my eyes to the fact that there was a whole other realm of healing and understanding that I had never explored. It was like a door had been opened to a new perspective, one that felt deeply personal and aligned with what I needed at that moment.

It felt like the universe was nudging me toward something new, and while I was healing, I began working with a new mentor to figure out my next career step. Strangely enough, during our conversations, the idea of starting my own business came up. I had spent 28 years in the corporate world, and this felt like a huge *aha* moment for me.

So, instead of focusing on my next steps in the corporate world, I started exploring what type of business I could create—something that aligned with my passions. What became clear was that I wanted to use my wisdom and kindness to support women in fulfilling their dreams and goals. I wanted to create a space where women could take a break, refresh themselves, and be part of a community without judgment or guilt. That's how Your Sanctuary Space, a women's retreat business, came to life.

What I learned during the coming months in 2023 while starting my side business, working full-time in my corporate role, and continuing my spiritual journey was profound. For the first time, I realised that success doesn't have to come at the expense of my health. I had been running on overdrive, constantly in survival mode, working from a place of masculine energy—force, control, and action. I'd always felt that in order to succeed in the corporate world, I had to push, compete, and constantly *do*. What I discovered through my healing was that this approach was no longer serving me. My body was telling me to slow down, to listen, to nurture, and to *be* rather than do—being in my feminine energy.

As I began to dive into spirituality, I was introduced to energy healing which became a lifeline for me, helping me reconnect with my body and soul in a way I hadn't before. It wasn't just about healing the physical exhaustion I was feeling, it was about going deeper, addressing emotional wounds that I had carried for years—some of which I hadn't even realised were there.

The more I explored, the more I realised that much of what I was carrying wasn't just my own pain. It was the result of generational trauma—ancestral restrictions passed down through the women in my family. I started to recognise the patterns: the limiting beliefs, the self-sacrifice, the need to always be strong and resilient without ever showing vulnerability, the need to be seen and not heard, people please and avoid conflict at all costs. These were ancestral wounds that had been ingrained in me, and for the first time, I was able to see them for what they were.

Through inner child healing, I began to connect with the younger version of myself—the girl who had learned to suppress her emotions, to prioritise others over herself, and to strive for perfection. I started to understand that much of my life had been shaped by these subconscious beliefs, and the only way to break free was to heal that little girl. Reiki and other forms of energy work allowed me to release these deep-rooted blocks, giving me the space to finally step into a new way of being.

One of the biggest revelations during this time, and particularly during this year, 2024, since leaving the corporate world at the end of 2023 when I was made redundant (a blessing in disguise), was realizing how much I had been operating from a masculine energy space for most of my life. In the corporate world, I had learned to embody qualities like structure, control, and action—all of which are necessary but have taken over my way of being. I didn't know how to allow myself to flow, to soften, and to trust my intuition. This was my feminine energy, something I had neglected for so long, and it impacted my personal life as well as my professional life.

As I healed, I understood the importance of balancing both energies within myself. The shift from always *doing* to allowing myself to *be* has been transformative. I now see the value in resting, receiving, and nurturing not only others but myself. Embracing my feminine energy has given me a sense of freedom I hadn't felt before, and it's allowed me to connect with other women on a much deeper level.

It's no coincidence that my business is now centred around helping women heal because I had to go through my own healing first to understand what true balance looks like. I am still working on this, and the more I learn myself, the more I am able to share with other women.

In March 2023, I soft-launched the business as a side hustle. I kept it quiet from work and many family and friends, because I knew it was something completely unexpected. I wasn't ready to answer the questions that would inevitably come, and I wasn't sure how this would go and where it would lead me. I quickly realised that while retreats were wonderful, and I loved seeing the positive and transformative impact they were having on the guests, they wouldn't generate the income I needed to support my family. I started thinking about other ways I could help women in the health and wellness space, and that's when I decided to become a coach.

By mid-2023, I was working toward my Coaching Diploma. I had been part of coaching and mentoring programs throughout my corporate career, both as a mentee and a mentor, so this felt like a natural next step for me. Since then, I've earned my Professional Coaching diploma, Life Coaching diploma, Reiki Level 1 and 2 certifications, and Mindfulness Teacher certification. I've also completed Oracle Card reading training, Women's Circle Facilitator training, and Sound Bowl Level 1 training. I'm planning to complete my Reiki Master certification and Sound Bowl Level 2 training later this year.

The transition from Corporate to deciding to focus full-time on my business this year hasn't been without challenges. Growing up in a conservative household and community, I wasn't always supported in my decisions. There have been expectations—both from family and friends—about how life should look, and I've had to push through limiting beliefs and imposter syndrome.

I've also faced scepticism from both men and women, in both personal and professional settings. But those experiences have only strengthened my resolve to help other women break free from similar expectations, and I'm determined not to allow them to hold me back.

Now, Your Sanctuary Space has evolved into a holistic healing business that offers Reiki, Life Coaching, and Retreats to women who need healing and support. I also recently launched my first digital product, a Mindfulness Challenge, to help women learn how to stay present and find their inner calm in six short weeks.

Interestingly, throughout 2024, I have continually received signs guiding me toward helping women in the corporate world, which, given my extensive background, makes perfect sense. Initially, I resisted these signs, as I was hesitant to return to the corporate environment in the same capacity as before. However, after recently delving into my Human Design and discovering that I am a Generator, it has become clear why the corporate space keeps resurfacing as part of my path. The consistent nudges I've received throughout this year have shown me that it's an area I need to re-engage with—but from a fresh perspective that aligns with my current journey and values.

As I reflect on my corporate career, I remember the moments when I wished someone had been there to guide me through the transition from being an employee to stepping into managerial and leadership roles. Now, I want to be that guide for other women—to empower them with insights and tools that I lacked, so they can navigate their paths with confidence.

My goal is to support women in creating a career that is both authentic and sustainable, helping them achieve success by incorporating a well-being approach, thereby reducing the risk of burnout. This renewed purpose excites me, and I look forward to sharing my experiences to uplift and inspire women to thrive in their corporate journeys.

I never could have predicted this path for myself, but every part of this journey has been transformative and fulfilling. It feels aligned with who I am, and I'm genuinely excited to see where it leads next. Stay tuned, as there is always so much more to come in all of our journeys.

SCAN TO MEET TANIA

# DR. MICHELLE MARIE LAPPIN
## INHERITANCE, DEBT & FINANCIAL STABILITY

Despite enduring childhood hardships like moving away from my father (not his choice), losing a loved one, experiencing multiple forms of abuse, and being a high school dropout, I've always held onto my dreams. Life had other plans, though, with financial challenges that tested my resilience to the core.

It started with a job shift that didn't go as planned, leading to mounting debt and unexpected expenses. The looming mortgage felt like a suffocating weight. I found myself spiraling downward, trapped in a financial abyss.

The darkest days were those spent navigating the short sale process, counting pennies, and worrying about how I'd put food on the table. The shame of needing assistance was a constant reminder of my mother's struggles growing up, a cycle I vowed to break.

I remember the sinking feeling in my stomach as I sat in the chair at the food bank for the first time. It was a stark contrast to the life I had once envisioned.

It was during this time of hardship that I discovered my inner strength. I realized that I couldn't let my circumstances define me. I had to take control of my financial future. I began to educate myself, devouring books on personal finance, budgeting, and investing. I created a strict budget, cut unnecessary expenses (even if it felt temporary), and started building an emergency fund, one penny at a time.

The road to recovery sometimes felt long and arduous. There were setbacks, frustrations, and moments when I questioned my ability to overcome these challenges. But I persevered, fueled by a burning desire to create a better life for myself and my son.

Slowly but surely, I saw progress. My debt shrank, my savings grew, and I felt more in control of my finances. Sharing my journey online inspired others to reach out for help. Some even asked why I wasn't offering financial guidance professionally. Intrigued, I realized the need for more people like me to help others. With newfound financial stability and support, I pursued my entrepreneurial dreams.

With the support of a dear friend and mentor, I launched my own business, leveraging my newfound financial knowledge and skills to help others navigate their own financial journeys. My personal experience gave me a unique perspective on the struggles people face, having been there myself. I was passionate about empowering others to achieve financial freedom and break free from the cycle of debt.

Through my business, I've been able to provide personalized financial guidance and support to countless individuals. I've helped clients create budgets, pay off debt, build emergency funds, and invest for their future. Seeing the positive impact my work has had on my clients' lives is incredibly rewarding.

I believe that everyone deserves to have control over their finances and live a life free from worry and stress. My goal is to continue empowering others to achieve financial freedom and build a brighter future.

While my financial journey has been significant, it's not the only area where I've faced adversity. I've also had to overcome personal challenges, including mental health issues, abuse, family dynamics, and the unique demands of single motherhood in the military.

One of the biggest challenges I faced was dealing with anxiety and depression. These conditions can be debilitating, making it difficult to function and enjoy life. However, with the help of therapy, faith, and a strong support system, I was able to manage my symptoms and find coping mechanisms that worked for me.

Family dynamics have been another challenge. While some family members have been a source of love and support, others have not. My father, however, has always been a constant source of support and encouragement. He has been there for me through thick and thin, offering me unconditional love and guidance.

I've also been incredibly fortunate to have a close friend who has become like a sister to me. She has been a source of support, friendship, and laughter throughout my life. Having her by my side has made a huge difference.

Learning to communicate effectively and set boundaries has been crucial in maintaining healthy relationships with my family. It's important to surround yourself with people who uplift and support you.

As a military mother with a military ex-partner, I've faced the challenges of long-distance parenting and solo motherhood. Juggling work, parenting, and household responsibilities has been demanding, but I've learned to prioritize and delegate tasks to make my life easier. Throughout my journey, I've learned the importance of self-care and taking time for myself. Whether it's spending time in nature, practicing mindfulness, or simply taking a relaxing bath, self-care is essential for maintaining my mental and emotional well-being.

One of the most challenging aspects of my journey has been forgiving those who have hurt me. I've experienced multiple forms of abuse, both emotional and physical, and it has taken me years to heal from the pain.

Forgiveness is not about condoning someone's actions or forgetting what they've done. It's about releasing yourself from the anger, resentment, and bitterness that can hold you back.

Through therapy, meditation, and prayer, I've been able to work through my anger and resentment. I've learned to forgive those who have hurt me, not for their sake, but for my own. Forgiveness has allowed me to find peace and move on with my life.

Overcoming these challenges has been a journey of self-discovery and personal growth. While I've made significant progress, I'm not always perfect at applying the techniques I've learned. In new environments or under stress, I might find myself reverting to old habits.

Despite these setbacks, I've learned that I am stronger and more resilient than I ever thought possible. I've also learned the importance of seeking help when needed and surrounding myself with a supportive network of people.

One of the most valuable lessons I've learned is the power of gratitude. Focusing on the positive aspects of my life has helped me to cultivate a more optimistic outlook and overcome adversity. I've also learned the importance of setting goals and taking small, achievable steps towards them. Breaking down large goals into smaller, more manageable tasks can help you stay motivated and make progress.

One of the most significant turning points in my journey was the realization that my mindset played a crucial role in my success. For years, I had been trapped in a negative thought cycle, constantly focusing on my shortcomings and limitations. This negative mindset was holding me back from achieving my goals and living a fulfilling life.

I began to make a conscious effort to shift my mindset towards a more positive and empowering one. I started practicing gratitude, focusing on the good things in my life, and challenging negative thoughts. I also sought out inspirational resources, such as books, podcasts, and motivational speeches, to help me cultivate a more positive outlook.

Over time, my mindset began to shift. I started to see myself in a new light, believing in my abilities and potential. This newfound confidence gave me the courage to take risks, pursue my dreams, and overcome challenges.

Self-doubt is a common challenge that many people face. It can hold us back from achieving our goals and reaching our full potential. Overcoming self-doubt requires self-awareness, self-compassion, and a willingness to challenge negative thoughts.

One of the most effective strategies for overcoming self-doubt is to focus on your strengths and accomplishments. Remind yourself of your past successes and the challenges you've already overcome. This can help boost your confidence and belief in yourself.

It's also important to challenge negative thoughts and replace them with positive affirmations. Instead of telling yourself: "I can't do this," try saying, "I can achieve anything I set my mind to."

Gratitude has been a cornerstone of my journey to healing and recovery.

During my darkest days, when I felt overwhelmed by challenges and self-doubt, focusing on the small blessings in my life was a lifeline.

I made a conscious effort to spend a few minutes each day expressing gratitude. Initially, it felt forced, but over time, it became a natural part of my routine. I would start my day by thanking God for waking me up, for giving me breath, and for providing me with shelter and food. As my circumstances improved, I continued to practice gratitude, focusing on the progress I had made and the positive changes in my life. I would thank God for the opportunities I had been given, for the people who supported me, and for the strength and resilience I had discovered within myself.

Practicing gratitude had a profound impact on my mindset. It helped me shift my focus from the negative to the positive, cultivating a more optimistic outlook. When I felt overwhelmed by challenges, I would remind myself of all the things I was grateful for, and it would help me regain my perspective.

Gratitude also helped me to appreciate the simple things in life that we often take for granted. It made me more mindful of the beauty and abundance around me.

I encourage you to incorporate gratitude into your daily life. Start by taking a few minutes each day to reflect on the things you're grateful for. You can also keep a gratitude journal or write a gratitude letter to someone who has made a positive impact on your life. The benefits of practicing gratitude are immeasurable, and it can be a powerful tool for healing, growth, and overall well-being.

Surrounding myself with a supportive network of people has been instrumental in my success. Having people who believe in you and encourage you to reach your goals can make a world of difference.

I was fortunate to have a few close friends and family members who were always there for me, offering support, encouragement, and advice. I also joined a support group for people who were struggling with similar challenges. Connecting with others who understood what I was going through was incredibly helpful and empowering.

Building a strong support network takes time and effort. It's important to be authentic and genuine in your relationships. Be open and honest about your needs, and don't be afraid to ask for help when you need it.

Goal setting played a pivotal role in my journey to financial recovery. When I was at my lowest, feeling overwhelmed by debt and uncertainty, setting clear goals provided a much-needed beacon of hope.

I started by defining my long-term financial goals. I wanted to be debt-free, build an emergency fund, and invest for my future. These goals gave me a sense of direction and purpose. Breaking down these large goals into smaller, more manageable steps was crucial. I created a detailed financial plan, outlining specific actions I needed to take to achieve my goals. This plan provided a roadmap and kept me focused on the path ahead.

One of my most significant financial goals was to pay off my credit card debt. I created a debt repayment plan, focusing on paying off the card with the highest interest rate first. This strategy provided a sense of accomplishment as I saw my debt gradually decrease.

As I made progress towards my financial goals, I experienced a surge of motivation and confidence. It was a powerful reminder that with dedication and perseverance, anything is possible.

Setting goals not only provided direction but also helped me stay accountable. When I faced challenges or setbacks, I could refer back to my goals and remind myself of why I was working so hard.

I encourage you to set your own financial goals and create a plan to achieve them. Remember, the journey to financial freedom is a marathon, not a sprint. Stay focused, be patient, and celebrate your progress along the way.

My story is a testament to the power of resilience, determination, and the human spirit. I've faced significant challenges, but I've persevered and emerged stronger.

Through my work as a financial coach and mentor, I've helped countless individuals achieve financial freedom and break free from the cycle of debt. I'm passionate about empowering others and making a positive impact on the world.

Over the past six years, I've been inspiring others to overcome their own obstacles and achieve their dreams. I've shared my experiences, provided guidance, and offered practical tools to help people take control of their finances.

My goal is to continue empowering individuals and making a difference in their lives.

Throughout my journey, I've found that words can be incredibly powerful tools for motivation, encouragement, and inspiration. When I was facing my darkest moments, quotes and scripture provided me with the strength and hope I needed to persevere.

Here are some quotes that have helped me on my journey:

> "The greatest glory in living lies not in never falling, but in rising every time we fall." —Nelson Mandela

> "Believe you can and you're halfway there." —Theodore Roosevelt

> "The only person you are destined to become is the person you decide to be." —Ralph Waldo Emerson

> "Don't let yesterday use up too much of today." —Will Rogers

> "The best time to plant a tree was twenty years ago. The second best time is now." —Chinese Proverb

In addition to these quotes, I've found the Scriptures to be a source of inspiration and motivation.

Proverbs 13:11: "A rich man's wealth is his strong city, but the poverty of the poor is their ruin."

Proverbs 21:20: "The wise man's wealth is his crown, but the folly of fools is their ruin."

Deuteronomy 8:18: "But remember the Lord your God, for it is he who gives you the power to get wealth. He is the one who makes you successful."

Using quotes and scripture can be a powerful way to stay motivated and focused on your goals. I encourage you to find quotes and verses that resonate with you and keep them as a reminder of your strength and resilience. Remember, words have the power to shape our thoughts, beliefs, and actions. By surrounding yourself with positive and inspiring words, you can create a more fulfilling and meaningful life.

My story is a testament to the power of resilience, determination, and the human spirit. I've faced significant challenges, but I've persevered and emerged stronger. I believe that everyone has the potential to achieve financial freedom and live a fulfilling life.

Remember, you're not alone in this journey. Many people face financial challenges, but you're not defined by your circumstances.

I hope my story has inspired you to believe in your own potential and to never give up on your dreams. Now is the time to take action and start building your brighter financial future.

## HERE ARE SOME PRACTICAL STEPS TO GET YOU STARTED:

**Create a budget:** Track your income and expenses to identify areas where you can save money. Use budgeting tools or apps to simplify this process.

**Pay off debt:** Prioritize paying off high-interest debt, such as credit cards. Consider using the debt snowball method, where you pay off your smallest debts first to gain momentum.

**Build an emergency fund:** Aim to save at least 3–6 months of living expenses to cover unexpected costs like medical bills, job loss, or car repairs.

**Start investing:** Investing can help your money grow over time. Consider investing in stocks, bonds, mutual funds, or exchange-traded funds (ETFs).

**Stocks:** Represent ownership in a company. They can be risky but also offer the potential for high returns.

**Bonds:** Debt instruments issued by governments or corporations. They are generally considered less risky than stocks but offer lower returns.

**Mutual funds:** Pooled investments that invest in a variety of stocks, bonds, or other assets. They offer diversification and professional management.

**Exchange-traded funds (ETFs):** Similar to mutual funds but trade on stock exchanges like individual stocks. They offer lower fees and more flexibility.

**Consider tax-advantaged retirement accounts:** Contribute to retirement accounts like a 401(k) or IRA to save for your future and potentially reduce your tax liability.

**Protect yourself with life insurance:** Life insurance can provide financial security for your loved ones in the event of your death. It can also offer living benefits, such as critical illness or long-term care coverage.

**Seek professional advice:** Consider working with a financial advisor to develop a personalized financial plan that aligns with your goals and risk tolerance.

Remember, the journey to financial freedom is not always easy, but it's definitely worth it. With the right mindset, tools, and support, you can achieve your financial goals and create a brighter future for yourself and your loved ones.

SCAN HERE TO MEET MICHELLE

# LIZZY MORRIS

## MOTHERHOOD, HOME BIRTHS & ACTIVISM

In early 2020, after two years of endless disappointment, I finally saw the word I'd been waiting for: pregnant. The positive digital pregnancy test stared back at me, and my heart pounded in disbelief.

I am actually pregnant.

These words repeated in my mind for days, weeks, and even months after, as I tried to grasp the reality of what I'd longed for over the past two years. Though I knew two years wasn't the longest journey to motherhood, it had felt endless, and the constant negative tests had worn down my hope.

Finally, after all the tears and frustration, I was pregnant. I was beyond grateful. I was also convinced that the hardest part was behind me. Trying to conceive had been a painful, emotional rollercoaster, and I thought pregnancy would be the beginning of a smoother ride. Little did I know that I had barely scratched the surface of the challenges that awaited me.

From the start, I had a belief in birth that I had carried with me my entire life. I wasn't afraid of the process itself. My mother had ingrained in me the idea that birth was natural and that my body was fully capable of it. She'd given birth naturally, and always assured me that I could do the same—even with big babies, even without medication. This confidence in my body was something I clung to, something nobody could take from me. I was fascinated by birth and watched countless birth videos, everything from hospital inductions to unassisted RV births.

But even though I had this deep-seated belief that my body could handle birth, I dismissed the idea of a unsurveillanced home birth for myself. I was haunted by my own internalized fatphobia, the voice in my head that told me I wasn't the kind of woman who could do that. I convinced myself that no one would support a woman my size giving birth at home, as if I even needed their approval.

So, from the very beginning, I found myself in conflict with my own beliefs, making choices based on what I thought society, my family, and the medical world expected of me. My pregnancy progressed, and I surrendered to the medical model of care without question.

I went to every appointment, agreed to every test, and followed every protocol, not because I truly believed they were necessary, but because I didn't have the confidence to question them.

I didn't know enough about the hierarchy within the maternity care system to understand the dynamics at play, and my natural response, shaped by years of trauma, was to be a people pleaser.

I wanted to be a "good patient," and so I complied.

As my pregnancy advanced, I started having issues with my blood pressure. I suspected it was white coat syndrome, especially given the added stress of navigating doctor's appointments during the height of COVID-19. The constant masks, temperature checks, and health screenings made each appointment feel cold and impersonal. But instead of questioning the need for all the extra tests and scans, I submitted.

At 34 weeks, I went in for what I thought was just another routine appointment. My OB, who I hadn't seen in weeks due to her schedule, walked in and said calmly, "So, protocol says we induce at 37 weeks." I was stunned. Tears filled my eyes, and I began shaking uncontrollably. Somehow, despite all the monitoring and tests, I had convinced myself that I would easily make it to 42 weeks. Induction was never part of my plan.

My intuition screamed at me: *She's going to C-section you.* I just knew it. And yet, when I asked why she wanted to induce me, her answer was vague: "Risk factors." She didn't give me statistics, options, or a deeper explanation—just risk factors. That phrase stuck in my mind, and my internalized fatphobia took over. Of course, I need to be induced. I'm obese, and my blood pressure is high. Women like me are too high-risk to give birth without assistance. I rationalized the decision, despite every fiber of my being telling me that this wasn't the path I wanted to go down.

I entered the induction process in disbelief. It didn't feel real. It didn't feel like the way my birth was supposed to unfold. Three days later, after enduring excruciating pitocin-induced contractions, I asked for an epidural. I hadn't planned on one, but I couldn't take the pain anymore. I was physically and emotionally exhausted, and the epidural provided much-needed relief.

For the first time in days, I slept. But when I woke up in the middle of the night, something was wrong. All of my medications had been turned off, and my contractions had stopped. I pressed the call button, confused. The nurse informed me that a C-section had already been scheduled for 7 a.m. I was heartbroken. I couldn't understand why my induction had been stopped without anyone waking me, why no one had told me about the decision to proceed with surgery while I slept.

The C-section was a blur of fear and loneliness. I lay on the operating table, naked and vulnerable, surrounded by strangers. I felt completely alone. As they prepped me for surgery, I knew that I never wanted to experience anything like this again. I promised myself that my next birth would be different. But in that moment, I felt utterly powerless.

When my son was born, there was no instant flood of joy.

Instead, I felt numb, traumatized by the process that had brought him into the world. Our hospital stay was extended due to complications with his health, and breastfeeding was a struggle. Though I eventually fell in love with my baby and was beyond grateful to finally be a mother, I couldn't shake the trauma of his birth. It lingered in the back of my mind, haunting me.

Over time, I began to speak about my next potential birth in a different way. I'd tell people:

"I don't care if nobody supports me, I'll birth my baby in the backyard."

Yet, despite these bold declarations, my actions didn't align with my words. I was still stuck in a pattern of people-pleasing and giving my power away.

Just ten months after my son was born, I found myself pregnant again. This time, the pregnancy wasn't planned, but it wasn't a total surprise either. I immediately hired a home birth midwife, thinking this was the obvious solution after my traumatic hospital experience. I had heard that midwives were the saviors of VBAC (vaginal birth after C-section) mothers, and I believed that midwifery care would be the answer to all my problems.

However, this pregnancy was much harder than my first. I was diagnosed with hyperemesis gravidarum (HG), a severe form of morning sickness that lasted throughout my pregnancy. For months, I was violently ill, throwing up to the point where I would lose control of my bladder and bowels. I was constantly exhausted and humbled by the intensity of the sickness.

Despite the physical toll, I managed to gain nearly 20 pounds by the end of the pregnancy, and my firstborn, thankfully, was calm and adaptable during those months of chaos. But emotionally, I was unraveling.

During this pregnancy, I became obsessed with birth. I read books, watched documentaries, and absorbed as much information as I could. I was determined to have a different experience this time. But despite my growing knowledge, I started to notice red flags with my midwives.

Early in the third trimester, I began monitoring my blood sugar and felt proud of how well I was managing it with my diet. Yet, when I shared my numbers with the midwives, they focused on one slightly elevated reading after a Mexican meal and joked, "Looks like no more Mexican food for you!" No one mentioned a diagnosis of gestational diabetes, but I was told to keep monitoring my blood sugar. It felt unnecessary, but I complied, once again thinking that this was just the way things were for someone like me—someone in a bigger body.

Then came concerns about my fundal height, which was measuring ahead. I found the whole process absurd, especially since I was a woman of size and had lost a significant amount of weight prior to getting pregnant, leaving me with loose skin that distorted measurements. I knew it didn't make sense, but once again, I didn't speak up.

As my pregnancy progressed, my midwives grew increasingly alarmed. They falsely claimed that my baby could have a fatal heart condition, sending me to a high-risk specialist who then played the dead baby card. Panic attacks became a regular part of my life, but I didn't fire the midwives. I had invested thousands of dollars in their care, and I felt trapped.

By the time I reached 41 weeks, I was presented with an ultimatum: induce for licensure purposes or birth alone. That's when I was told, for the first time, that I had gestational diabetes—a condition that should have risked me out of home birth long ago. I was furious because it was obvious to me their intentions behind how the information was being presented to me, but I didn't feel like I had any choice but to continue. I let them continue to touch my body, monitor my labor, and try various induction methods.

Labor finally began at home, but as I neared the end, the head midwife entered my kitchen and rummaged through my fridge. Then, she asked me to check my blood sugar while I was in transition, less than an hour away from giving birth. The disruption was jarring, and I could feel the energy of my labor shift. Still, I complied.

When it came time to monitor the baby's heart rate, I was forced onto my back. Up until that point, I had been laboring on my feet, swaying and moving as felt most natural to me. But now I had to lie down, just like during my first birth. It was torturous, the pain of the contractions intensified by the unnatural position, and I felt a familiar sense of helplessness creeping in.

The midwife listened to the baby's heartbeat and immediately called 911, claiming that the fetal heart tones were concerning. In my heart, I knew this intervention wasn't necessary, but I was too exhausted and too overwhelmed to fight it. Within minutes, I found myself strapped onto a stretcher, placed flat on my back, and loaded into an ambulance. I was being whisked away to the hospital, reliving the trauma I had experienced with my first birth, but this felt far worse.

The ride to the hospital was excruciating. Being forced to labor on my back was agony, and I felt completely out of control. Worse still, the midwife kept my doula behind to help her clean up at my house. She (the midwife) didn't come with me to the hospital, didn't call me, didn't check on me at all. I felt abandoned.

When I arrived at the hospital, I was naked, vulnerable, and surrounded by strangers once again. But this time, I wasn't quiet. I screamed. I demanded to be heard. I advocated for myself in every way I could, even though I was in the most intense pain of my life. Despite my best efforts, I was still violated. Hands touched my body without permission, and strangers barked orders at me. It was happening, all my fears had surfaced.

Despite all the chaos and trauma, I managed to give birth vaginally. It was a small victory, but the experience had once again been overshadowed by unnecessary interventions and the stripping away of my autonomy. Though I was grateful for my baby and proud to have avoided another C-section, I couldn't escape the trauma that clung to me.

In the weeks and months that followed, I struggled with severe postpartum anxiety and PTSD. I was afraid to tell people the truth about how I felt because I worried they would see me as ungrateful or that they'd judge me for being the "girl who can never be satisfied."

The trauma of my second birth also took a toll on my marriage. The constant anxiety, sleepless nights, and emotional overwhelm created a distance between my husband and me that was hard to bridge. We were both trying to cope with the aftershocks of the birth experience, but it felt like we were on separate islands, each dealing with our own pain.

Despite everything, I had always wanted more children. But after my second birth, I found myself wondering if two might be enough. The thought of going through that level of trauma again was too much to bear. I avoided processing the birth trauma fully because it felt like it was already too deeply woven into my daily life. And then, history repeated itself.

Eleven months postpartum, I found myself pregnant again. This time, the pregnancy was a complete surprise. I was in shock when I saw the positive test. I hadn't planned on having another child so soon, and the idea of facing pregnancy and birth again felt overwhelming. But this time, I knew one thing for certain: I couldn't make the same choices I had made before. If I wanted a different outcome, I had to walk a different path.

They say the definition of insanity is repeating the same actions and expecting different results, so I knew I needed to take a radically different approach this time around. I had to stop people-pleasing. I had to reclaim my autonomy over my body and my birth. I had to dig deep and figure out what I truly wanted, what my fears were, and how society's expectations had shaped my choices.

I made the decision to keep my pregnancy private, telling no one—not even family. I needed to drown out the noise. I couldn't afford to have other people's opinions, fears, or judgments influencing my choices. This pregnancy wasn't about appeasing others; it was about protecting my autonomy.

Physically, this third pregnancy was my hardest yet. The sickness was brutal, even worse than during my second pregnancy. But this time, I had two children to care for. My body was exhausted from three back-to-back pregnancies in less than three years. My oldest child wasn't even three yet, and I was carrying the physical and emotional weight of it all.

But despite the physical difficulties, this pregnancy felt different. I wasn't under constant surveillance. There were no weekly appointments, no ultrasounds, no one looking over my shoulder. It gave me the space to reflect and figure out what really mattered to me.

After careful thought, I decided to freebirth this baby. I knew that if I truly wanted to protect my birth experience, I couldn't invite anyone else's fears or projections into the space. I needed to be in complete control, and the only person in the world I trusted to respect my autonomy was my husband.

We prepared for the birth together, working through the "what-ifs" and making sure we were both on the same page. This was also the first baby where we chose not to find out the gender beforehand, which added a fun element of surprise to the pregnancy. Though we were nervous about adding another child to our family so soon, by the end of the pregnancy, we began to feel more at ease and even started celebrating what was to come.

As the end approached, I finally shared the news of the pregnancy with a few family members. It was Christmas Eve, and I was 38 weeks pregnant. I felt confident that I would still be pregnant for a few more weeks. But as the universe often does, it had other plans.

Two weeks later, at exactly 40 weeks, my labor began. The timing couldn't have been more inconvenient. We were just a few days away from moving, and the apartment was filled with half-packed boxes. But despite the chaos,

I was excited. This birth was different. It was the one I had been looking forward to. I knew that this time, we would be untouched, undisturbed, and unharmed.

At first, I didn't even believe I was in labor. The contractions came every 10–15 minutes, and I convinced myself that this could go on for days. But I stayed in contact with my sister, who was the only other person I had invited into my birth space. She remained on standby, ready to be there if I needed her, but her presence over the phone was enough.

As the night wore on, the contractions intensified, and I finally accepted that labor was in full swing. Around 2 a.m., I woke my husband and told him that our baby would be here soon. For the next few hours, I walked around the apartment, swaying and moving with each contraction. My husband was my rock, literally holding me up and supporting me through each wave. Unlike in my previous births, this time, we were free to labor together, uninterrupted by anyone else.

Labor was intense and painful, but there was something incredibly empowering about being in my own space, surrounded by the love and oxytocin that filled the room. I wasn't afraid. I trusted my body and my baby. When I reached transition, my water broke, and I knew that the baby would be here any minute. I could feel my cervix opening as my baby moved down. With each contraction, I felt my baby's descent, and I marveled at the intricate, beautiful process of birth. I didn't need anyone to tell me what was happening or stick their hands inside me to check my progress. I knew my baby was coming, and I knew that we were safe.

After a few more intense contractions, my baby shot out into the world. My husband and our middle child were there to witness the moment, and it was my husband who got to be the first to see our baby. As I turned to meet my baby, I announced with joy, "It's a girl!" I couldn't believe it. My intuition had told me all along that I was carrying a girl, but after two boys, I was hesitant to trust that instinct. But there she was—our perfect baby girl.

The birth was everything I had hoped for: peaceful, undisturbed, and filled with love. For the first time in my motherhood journey, I felt completely whole. I hadn't been broken by the experience. Instead, I felt more intact and stronger than ever before.

I had told myself that a woman like me couldn't have this kind of birth, that it wasn't safe, but I had proven the girl on the left wrong. I had reclaimed my body, my autonomy, and my power.

Giving birth on my own terms had been a journey of self-discovery, teaching me to trust myself, to honor my boundaries, and to stand firm in what mattered most to me. My first two births had opened deep wounds— wounds of sexual trauma, shame, and mistrust. But my third birth healed those wounds. It gave me a new foundation of trust within my family, trust within my body, and a sacred way of bringing new life into the world.

For the first time in forever, I didn't feel shattered. I felt whole. This journey has never been easy, but it has always been worth it. And now, standing on the other side, I am eternally grateful for everything I learned, shed, and grieved through to get here.

SCAN TO MEET LIZZY

# KIMEIKO RAE VISION

## RESILIENCE, REFLECTION & NORTHERN LIGHTS

It was the spring of 2020, and suddenly, I had an abundance of time on my hands. With a mandate to "Shelter in Place," I found myself rediscovering knitting and crochet.

Digging through my closet to find a buried hobby, I unearthed an old set of silver aluminum knitting needles, still attached to a twenty-year-old skein of neon-orange yarn—the color of a traffic cone. Next to it was a much more peaceful ball of cotton yarn, hand-dyed in soft pastels: turquoise, magenta, emerald green, and gold. Let's be generous and call these "vintage."

These were my companions for the first six months of the COVID-19 pandemic. They kept me busy, entertained, and (surprisingly) calm.

Eventually, I ran out of yarn. I ventured to a nearby Hobby Lobby, a store I'd heard of but never really bothered to check out. I had somehow decided Hobby Lobby People weren't my people—likely because of a few soundbites about political tension and polarized echo chambers. But every time I visited, I was met with only kindness and cheerful attitudes from staff and customers alike! Even their decorative signs read "Positive Vibes Only."

Except for the last time.

I was in my tiny turquoise hybrid, patiently waiting for a parking spot, when a massive white Lincoln Town Car swooped in front of me, taking me right back to my childhood in Alaska when my parents had one. There were two women, with a baby in the car, making damn sure I saw their fury. I slowed to let them pass, smiling to show I was waiting patiently. They didn't smile back.

Instead, both of them glared at me, letting me know how angry they were.

Finally, the car backed into the spot. No problem on my end. Maybe it was my slow reaction time that made them so mad? I'll never know. I found my own spot, but as I walked toward the store, they re-engaged. They insulted me, dragged me into a confrontation, and tried to shame me in front of the baby with them.

It was bizarre. These women, with a baby in tow, were bullying me!

If that baby had any idea what was going on, they'd probably be more concerned about the erratic driving with minors in the car and the random bursts of rage aimed at unsuspecting strangers.

Now, I'm starting to lose my temper.

It felt strange walking toward the store in lockstep with these two-and-a-half strangers. This was ridiculous.

Once inside, they got louder, trying to humiliate me in front of the cashiers and people in line. Cornered, I could either act like a clown or be combative. Pitiful either way.

I chose to walk away and visit a store down the street, hoping they'd leave before I returned. But my blood was boiling. I felt so misunderstood and diminished. That's when I decided to use one of my oldest tricks: I took a deep breath and whispered, "Angels. Please. Help."

They have no idea what I'm going through right now.

I sulked for a minute, but then it hit me.

Instead of feeling solely wronged, I realized I had no idea what they were going through, either. Maybe they'd just lost someone at war. Maybe that baby's father was gone. Maybe one had just been laid off or was battling cancer. Maybe one had a stomach ache or a wedgie. I don't know.

It didn't matter. I was proud of myself for walking away. But once I calmed down, I felt ashamed for getting pulled into their drama.

It dawned on me: I try to give others the benefit of the doubt. I hope they'll do the same for me when I lose my cool. But those two women? They'd only ever see me as I was in that parking lot. And that stung.

What I do know is that it is one of my strongest values to be kind, even in the face of foolery or aggression that comes seemingly from nowhere, because you never know what a person is going through.

The incident struck a chord deep within me. It dredged up a very old story.

Yes. It did.

* * *

It's my first day of high school. It's nearing lunchtime, and I'm thinking, *I've MADE IT!* Halfway through the day, that is... I have just a few more hours here and then I get to go home!

After lunch, I head to my Government class. There are six rows of five desks. I'm in row 1, seat 2, which I scoped out specifically against a wall. I love the cool feeling of the white brick behind me—my small comfort.

The teacher walks out from behind her desk, wearing a floor-length denim skirt and a handcrafted silver belt buckle. This is paired with a dark t-shirt and vest with many cross-stitched kittens on it. She's passionate about voting, but I'm less than enthusiastic. I'm trying to give it a chance, at least a little.

She keeps my attention on raw passion, as this is one of her favorite classes to teach. "Alright, class! I have been a SUPER Voter the past 22 years and YOU should be too, because it makes a fantastic impact on the Institution of Government!"

She gets my attention with her fiery speech on the virtues of "voting," stressing how important it is for the next 45 minutes. Honestly? I didn't know there was so much to it.

...Aha!

I finally make the connection that's been driving me nuts: she looks and sounds just like Jodie Foster in *Maverick* and *Silence of the Lambs.*

By the time I've realized that, she's assigning homework. We're supposed to interview our parents about voting habits and write a few paragraphs on what they said. Simple, right?

"Alright, class, have this done by tomorrow... It is very important... We will be building on it throughout the rest of the year..."

In a perfect world, it would have been easy... Unfortunately for me, home wasn't always a place for perfection or ease. There is no time for my interviews or other homework.

Amid raised voices and shouting, my mom tells me to go to my room and close the door. I can't. I chase them through the house, begging them to stop. But they don't hear me. I stop using my voice, but inside, I'm still shouting:

*Please stop.*

*PLEASE.*

*Stop this!*

I felt untethered in a tumultuous storm at sea. I've been holding my breath. This could all go overboard at any moment.

Then, in desperation: *Angels. Please. Help.*

* * *

It's my second day of high school. The teacher walks around with a clipboard, stopping at my desk.

"Kimeiko, do you have your homework?"

Whoops. I forgot.

"No, I'm sorry."

She clicks her teeth in disapproval. TSK. "That's too bad... You're NOT going to graduate this class if you don't complete your homework."

I try to explain: "You said we'd be working on it all year, so I didn't think it was due today."

She's not having it. The stare-down continues.

After finally moving on to interrogate the other students, she resumes speaking poetically again about the virtues of voting before assigning more homework.

Later that day, I pass Ms. Judy on my way home to our third-floor condo. A few months ago, she introduced herself. She's that friendly neighbor with the thick Southern accent. Charming, but clearly here for more than small talk.

She knocks on our door confidently. She's concerned. She heard the noise from upstairs and wants me to know that if I ever need a safe place, I can come to her.

"Hi, honey! I'm your new downstairs neighbor. I just wanted to introduce myself. Your little girl helped me with my groceries the other day, and I... I just wanted to introduce myself! Haaiii! I'm Judy!"

She had sparkles in her eyes. Not only was Ms. Judy's bubbly small talk bearable, it was downright charming and enjoyable. Enchanting as she was, Ms. Judy fumbled through transitioning to the real reason she had stopped by...

"SO... that's pretty much all about me, and I know I've just about talked your ear off... but there was just... um, one more thing I wanted to say... I've noticed some rumblin' up here.

My mom, always polite, stops breathing, stiffens, and shifts her weight. I can tell she wants to slam the door, but Ms. Judy doesn't give up.

"No need to be embarrassed, honey. I've been through things too. If your little girl ever needs somewhere safe, just send her downstairs. We'll be ready for her."

My mom is silent, humiliated, but relieved to have Judy's offer.

Thank goodness for Ms. Judy's kindness, because that night, my parents' shouting match escalated. Furniture, doors, and walls are slammed. I call 911, and soon the police and EMTs are at our door. Their pounding makes me want to cover my ears.

Ugh. So... My second day of high school was one of those nights.

A super late evening that I got to go and "hang out" with my lovely downstairs neighbor, Ms Judy... Ms. Judy is doing her very best to make it seem like all we're really doing is having a good old-fashioned sleepover at her house.

She's made a place for me to sleep on the couch with smooth, crisp fresh sheets, puffy cloud-like pillows, and wonderfully frilly quilted pillow shams. Clean and white. Fit enough for angels to sleep in. The setup is inviting. It is so late. But I'm on edge. I can't just lie down.

Outside, multiple car doors to multiple vehicles are opened and shut. One of the police cars leaves with Dad inside. An ambulance leaves with Mom in tow. Inside, there's another uncomfortably powerful knock at the door.

Ugh.

A pair of police officers come in.

Their shiny black steel-toed boots are tracking in soil from outside stepping over the carpet. Ms Judy's light beige carpet is so clean, so fluffy and light. I find these dirty footprints in Ms Judy's pristinely clean home to be offensive. I'm offended.

This is the only emotion besides terror and confusion that I've felt for hours. One of them informs Ms. Judy of the updates. Which jailhouse and which hospital my parents can be found in, tomorrow. The other officer thanks her for watching over me. Tells her I'm lucky to have her, so close by, as one of my angels. "Oh!" She says. "I'm lucky to have this little one come to hang out with me for a bit! She's wonderful! So smart and so funny!"

The police leave, and she gently closes the door behind them. She gives me a great big hug. Ms. Judy has to work in the morning. She knows I have school and can get myself there, and it's probably the best place that I can go. I finally get to go back upstairs. But first:

"Here, take this with you, kiddo. Just in case you need another squeeze."

She hands me a teddy bear as a gift to keep me company upstairs.

Walking back into my apartment, the door frame is damaged, but I do my best to close it behind me. Good enough for now. I feel ridiculous, carrying a fresh teddy bear through this deserted domestic war zone. I don't turn on any lights. Any clean-up from tonight's tribulations must happen later. Even in the dark, I can see spots of blood on the linoleum floor, crossing the boundary from the kitchen onto the carpet in the hallway. This stupid, ugly, messy carpet.

Adding to the growing list of physical imperfections in my home the evidence of dysfunction and terror, a further fall from grace.

In my bedroom, back at home, I feel lost at sea. So many different waves of emotions are rocking me, and the ground beneath my feet feels unsteady. My hands are clenched. There's no one to comfort me now when I need it the most. Ms. Judy tried, but I couldn't bear the pity in her eyes. We both knew it was better to let me retreat to my own home.

I am pitiful, though, aren't I? I'm just a damn trashy loser.

I sit rigid, tense, like a giant iceberg bobbing in the dark waters of the Kenai Fjords, alone and cold. Silent tears fall, chasing each other down my cheeks. A distant voice whispers—drowned out, but something about "light" or "night"? I imagine the rush of water past the fjords, embracing the sound. With this auditory experience, I'm aware of my trembling body and how my forehead feels so heavy and my face so hot. It all intensifies the illusion.

The cold Alaskan night presses against my window, and I push my nose, then chin, to the glass. An angry, salty breath escapes, fogging up the surface. I trace a stick figure, add in wings, and then sketch a moon to go with it. The little halo over the figure is so novel that it almost makes me smile—my very own guardian angel, imagined in the fog.

But I'm not allowed to smile. Not on a night like tonight. Is my mom going to be okay? I don't know. I'm exhausted.

I sit on my Sashiko hand-embroidered comforter at the foot of my four-post bed, feeling fragile. My lavender walls feel like they could crumble, and so could I. The room radiates coolness, while I still feel hot and messy like a bucket full of charcoal. I could melt right through this wall.

Or collapse through the floor.

Maybe bring the whole place down with me.

What am I supposed to do?

The tiny voice returns: *Give yourself the tears, Little One. Let yourself rest. It's okay. You can go to sleep.*

I glance up and over my right shoulder, my little angel drawn onto the glass, is nearly invisible now that my breathy fog has evaporated. But I can tell that my angel *is* still there.

*Keep your chin up, Little One... Eyes on the northern lights.*

So, I lift my chin and raise my eyes. Oh, wow. Aurora Borealis. Mysterious. Majestic. Unmistakable. Dancing in the sky, turquoise, magenta, emerald green, bits of gold. In stripes and striations, like the yarn my mommy helped me pick out. She's going to teach me how to knit soon. I already have my supplies.

I love the northern lights. A beautiful light show provided by Mother Nature herself. Nature's fireworks. I welcome the distraction. I probably wouldn't have noticed them if not for that still small voice. I find gratitude creeping in, pushing back the turmoil.

I squeeze the teddy bear Ms. Judy gave me, twisting it with all my sadness and anger. I unkindly strangled, twisted, and imbued my poor new toy with sorrow, hopelessness, confusion, anger, and utter despair.

I'm trying to comfort myself enough to calm down and go to sleep. It's not working. I feel so weak. If I can be strong, then maybe my family will be okay. Fighting tears back. My heart is still pounding.

Angels, please help me.

I take a deep breath. A wave of calm washes over me. I close my eyes, still seeing the northern lights in my mind. I can let go now. More tears flow, attacking my pillow and the teddy bear instead of my pride, face, and neck.

Thank you, Angels.

As I fall asleep, I think... *Just a few more hours... and then I get to go back to school.*

* * *

It's my third day of high school, and I've already failed to bring my homework... Again.

The teacher shakes her head, clicks her tongue, and tells me, "You're NOT going to pass this class, and you NEED this class to graduate."

Ouch. I'm crushed. Shocked. Horrified that on day three of my high school experience, she's already predicting not only will I fail her class, but I won't graduate at all!

I understand that she couldn't have known what I was facing at home. Regardless, the hurt she doled out was long-lasting. Causing multiple invisible scars.

I remember thinking, *Seriously? Because I forgot homework for two days, now I'm a failure? LADY?! Are you kidding me?*

Oh, I get it... You just think I'm lazy and not paying attention, huh?

I've already failed you, and you're not seeing me as a productive student and, therefore, probably not a productive member of society.

I didn't remember much else from that class. No lessons, no faces of classmates, just her words echoing in my head.

Three months later... I didn't pass that class.

Four years later... I didn't graduate high school.

And for two decades, I heard those words daily: "You're NOT going to graduate..."

My teacher had predicted and declared my failure, looking down on me from her teacher's pedestal, after barely even glancing at my potential. I heard those words play in my head every single day as I moved through life, taking shifts terrorizing both my conscious and subconscious mind. They reminded me of that quick judgment, of my own perceived uselessness.

Until recently, I let them silence me. I hid and shut myself away from life.

But not anymore.

I've always been the empath, the healer, the court jester—skills I needed growing up to survive at home. Today, I'm a FABULOUS Live Event Emcee, speaking to hundreds or thousands, bringing authenticity, humor, and connection. I'm a problem solver, a teacher, and a leader, helping others discover their people and their potential.

Today, I am helping others even as I am still healing.

I'm an entertainer and a guide. I strive to immerse audiences in awe, wonder, open-heartedness, and community. I understand now that belief in someone can change everything. I understand that someone believing in you and making sure that you feel safe has a powerful effect on learning. That's what I bring to the events I emcee at multi-speaker events with my colleagues. I prioritize people feeling safe to learn, excel, grow, and be themselves.

I wish I could tell that little girl in Alaska, staring up at the northern lights, struggling in the darkness, that she was NOT stupid, or a loser, or a waste of effort.

She wasn't a pitiful sorry sight, either.

She has inherent value that she'll continue to discover her value and purpose and joy with TRUTH, LOVE, AND COMPASSION that only grows more and more, each day, year, and decade that passes by.

That teacher probably hasn't thought of me since the '90s. But sometimes, I wonder if she knew where I am now… would she be proud? I think she might. I think she'd really get a kick out of the fact that, even more importantly, I have also become a SUPER Voter.

But honestly, whether she would be proud of me or not…

I am proud of myself.

There will always be haters who want to try to criticize you, nitpick, oppress, diminish, or defame you. In your own head, there may be cobwebs and echoes of past situations and tiny, hurtful voices you've unknowingly adopted.

There are nefarious buzzards who will steal your joy, steal your credit, steal your ideas or intellectual property. They'll talk smack about you to anyone who'll listen. They sell it to the highest or the lowest bidder, and put it up for sale on the internet or the sidewalk, shamelessly.

Pay them no mind. Do YOUR thing.

We cannot ever stop the haters from doing what they do best. #hating

What you can do is protect your peace. Promise yourself you'll never let the voices of haters occupy more of your time or mental energy than your angels, your highest self, and your Higher Power.

I hope you sleep well tonight!

Angel Blessings,
Kimeiko Rae Vision
The Angel Warrior

**SCAN TO MEET KIMEIKO**

# AMANDA CHATZIKONSTANTINOU
## ANXIETY, NOT-ENOUGH-NESS & TEEN SUPPORT

As a teenager, I struggled with anxiety, depression, and the overwhelming pressure of trying to figure out who I was. It felt like there was this constant weight on my shoulders—like I had to be perfect or have it all figured out. At the time, no one talked openly about mental health, so I had no words for what I was experiencing. I didn't even know what I was going through was a "thing." I just felt like I was drowning in my own thoughts and emotions. I thought I was the only one who felt this way, so I kept it all inside because I didn't know how to ask for help.

Luckily my family was supportive, and I had really amazing friends, but somehow, I still felt isolated. Because no one could see the pain I was carrying, I struggled in silence. I didn't know where to turn or how to start healing. I didn't have a coach. I didn't have a therapist. I didn't have someone who could just sit with me and say:

"I get it, you're not alone."

Much later, when I began my personal growth journey, I realized how much that lack of resources shaped who I became. But that difficult time in my life didn't define me—it propelled me. I eventually discovered how life-changing it is to have someone to guide you through those pivotal years, someone who could offer perspective, understanding, and the tools to cope.

Now, let me take you back to 10th grade.

I vividly remember standing at my locker, getting ready for my next class. The hallways were quiet since everyone was already in class. Then, all of a sudden, I started feeling... off. I could feel the heaviness in my chest, the tightness in my throat, and the panic rising. My heart started racing like it was training for a marathon. Everything got blurry and started spinning.

I tried to shake it off. "Just breathe," I kept telling myself.

(Spoiler: It didn't work.)

The room felt like it was closing in, and before I knew it, everything went black. My legs gave out. The next thing I remember, I was lying on the cold hallway floor, paramedics all around me, asking questions I couldn't even begin to answer. My mind was completely blank. I couldn't figure out what was happening to me, but I knew one thing for sure: something was very wrong. It felt like my body had just given up, and I was powerless to stop it.

The doctors ran every test they could think of, trying to find an explanation, but nothing came back abnormal. I should've felt relieved, right? Nope! Instead, all I could think about was... how could that be true when my body clearly disagreed? When deep down I could feel something wasn't right! That disconnect between what they were saying and what I was experiencing was incredibly frustrating, confusing, and, honestly, kind of scary.

The hardest part? This wasn't a one-time event. It happened again! And again! I was stuck in this loop—something felt deeply wrong, but no one could tell me what it was. My body felt completely out of control, and the fact that I didn't know why made it even worse. It left me feeling completely powerless.

It was like my body had a mind of its own, running wild, and I couldn't keep up. The uncertainty was crushing, and since I didn't know when the next episode would strike, I was trapped in a cycle of fear and confusion. It was like a ticking time bomb, never knowing when it would go off!

For a while, I didn't talk to anyone about it because, honestly, I didn't even know what to say. On the outside, it looked like I was fine—getting straight As in my classes and volunteering at any chance I got (especially when it meant I got to work with kids). I got accepted into university, and I had amazingly supportive friends and family. But on the inside, I was falling apart, and for a while, I just accepted it because I didn't really know what else to do.

I got really tired of this being "normal" for me, so I decided enough was enough, and I became very determined to figure it out. If doctors couldn't give me answers, I'd find my own.

Back then, mental health wasn't in casual conversations or school assemblies, and it certainly wasn't something I understood. Once I started researching and learning more, I realized something that shook me: I wasn't the only one feeling this way. A lot of my friends had experienced similar struggles, but none of us had been given the words or tools to explain it. We couldn't describe what we felt because we didn't even know what it was.

So, I dove even deeper into everything I could find about the brain, the nervous system, psychology... You name it! I became completely obsessed with understanding why my body was doing this to me and what was going on in my brain. The idea that my mind and body were connected was such a powerful new way for me, and it made so much sense. After a lot of searching, I finally found something: anxiety and panic attacks. It was like a light bulb went off. Suddenly, everything clicked. I finally knew what was happening, and naming it was a huge relief—it validated what I felt. I wasn't just "crazy" or imagining things. I wasn't broken! There was a reason behind it. My body wasn't betraying me—it was responding to something I didn't fully understand. There was finally an explanation for what I was going through! YAY!!!

But just knowing the reason didn't mean I was magically better. (I wish!) I still had to learn how to manage it, which took time and patience. Since, back then, mental health was something kind of whispered about but never addressed directly, I didn't have the vocabulary for what I was feeling, and I certainly didn't have tools to help me, either.

But, little by little, I started to figure it out. I learned ways to handle the panic attacks when they came on, and over time, I began to feel more in control of my body. It really felt like a huge victory. And for a while, it seemed I was doing much better. However, there was another layer to my story that I hadn't uncovered yet.

What could've been the end of my story turned out to be just the beginning.

I thought I'd done the hard part, that I was finally on the other side of the storm, and that everything was going to be smooth sailing from there. But what I didn't know at the time was that there was something deeper lurking beneath the surface—something I couldn't see then, but would eventually come to understand: my self-worth.

Looking back now, it's so clear. I'd gotten pretty good at managing the anxiety, but I hadn't learned how to truly love or value myself. And that's where everything started to unravel. Without that solid foundation of self-worth, I found myself in toxic (even abusive) relationships. At first, I didn't recognize the red flags. I convinced myself it was normal, that maybe it was my fault, that maybe I wasn't good enough to ask for more.

I thought if I just kept going, if I could push through it, things would eventually get better. But instead, I just kept accepting less than I deserved. I didn't believe I was worthy of anything more. I kept telling myself that if I just worked harder, if I just gave more, I could fix everything. I kept putting other people's needs before my own, bending over backward to make them happy, hoping that somehow, that would make things right. In the end, all it did was pull me further and further away from myself, and I felt totally lost (again!).

It took a couple more years and a lot of pain, before I finally realized what was really going on. I started journaling, pouring all my thoughts and feelings onto the page. At first, it was just a way to process the overwhelming mess in my mind. But over time, it became something more. As I wrote, it became painfully clear: the problem wasn't ever just anxiety. It went deeper than that. Deep down, I didn't believe I was worthy of love or respect.

YIKES! It was a tough pill to swallow, for sure. But in that moment of truth, things finally clicked. It was like everything I'd been struggling with suddenly made sense. It didn't make the pain go away, but it gave me clarity—a starting point for real change.

Those thoughts hit hard, but it also marked the start of real healing. It wasn't easy, and it didn't happen overnight, but it was exactly what I needed. Little by little, I learned to see my value, set boundaries, and build my self-worth— something I'd lost track of for so long.

For the first time, I really knew what it felt like to not feel broken. To not feel like I was falling apart. I felt validated. And that alone was huge. But knowing I wasn't broken didn't automatically mean I was healed. That was a whole different journey to take, one that required more time, more patience, and, honestly, a lot of self-compassion.

Through personal development, therapy, and diving into psychology, I discovered something life-changing: struggle can be the seed for growth. But as I sat with this new understanding, something else started to float around my brain. It made me wonder: Why wasn't anyone teaching us this? Why didn't someone sit me down and say, "Hey, what you're feeling is real, but it doesn't define you. You don't have to go through it alone. Here's how you can handle it." What if I'd known all of this sooner? What if someone had helped me understand what was going on with my mind and my body, what I was truly struggling with? What if I'd been given the tools to manage my anxiety, to love myself, to believe in myself before I hit rock bottom?

That's when it really hit me. That thought—that what-if—was a spark. It was the thing that set something bigger into motion within me. I didn't want anyone else to feel as lost and confused as I did. I didn't want them to go through all that pain alone, without any guidance. That's when I knew—this is what I was meant to do. I wanted to be the person who could help others avoid the struggle I had to endure, give them the tools and support I never had, and help them build a foundation of strength before they even needed it.

I look back now and realize, *If I hadn't gone through all of that, I wouldn't be so passionate about helping young people today.* My mission is clear now: to offer the guidance and support I wish I'd had back then. I want to be the person I needed when I was younger—I know how it feels to be lost, and I know how powerful it is to finally find your way. I want to give young people the tools to understand themselves, to love themselves, and to navigate life's challenges with confidence! That's how I ultimately found my way into life and wellness coaching.

Now, my mission is for every young person to have a coach, so they can see their potential and embrace their self-worth. I don't want them to feel like they have to struggle and figure it all out on their own, like I did. I want to give them the tools to be their best selves, to navigate anxiety, and to build the kind of confidence and self-love that will carry them through life. It's showing young people that they are worthy of love, respect, and happiness, no matter what!!

The work I do with teens is deeply rooted in a philosophy I've come to believe in wholeheartedly. I call it the "tree analogy."

If we look at ourselves as a garden, our thoughts, beliefs, and habits are like seeds. What we plant when we're young grows into the foundation of who we become. It's much easier to plant healthy seeds (like self-worth, resilience, and confidence) when we're young than it is to uproot a 50-year-old tree.

Think about it: A belief that's been growing for decades can be so deeply rooted that removing it feels nearly impossible. But if we plant the right seeds early, we can create a foundation that supports us for life. That's why I'm so passionate about working with young people. Helping them understand their worth, their potential, and their strength now can save them so much pain later.

Back then, I felt so lost and disconnected from the person I wanted to be. It was hard to see the strength I had in those moments, but now, looking back, I realize how resilient that version of me really was. And I want today's teens to see that same strength in themselves—no matter what they're facing.

Teen life can feel like juggling flaming swords—grades, social drama, family expectations, and the constant pressure to "be enough." Add the endless comparison games on social media, and it's no wonder teens feel overwhelmed and lost. That's where I step in as a coach. I work with teens to cut through the chaos and rediscover their inner superheroes. Together, we tackle self-doubt, communication struggles, and the big question of "Who am I?" This isn't about just making it through the teen years—it's about thriving. We build confidence, emotional resilience, and tools they'll carry for life. I help teens not only find their voice but also learn how to use it to create the future they deserve.

To the parents reading this: your support means everything. You don't have to have all the answers, but just being there and starting the conversation can make all the difference. My mission is to help make the journey a little smoother for the next generation, one conversation at a time. If you're ready to help your teen discover their inner strength, let's talk.

Looking back, my journey wasn't easy, but I'm incredibly grateful for it. My journey has taught me so much! Every challenge, every setback, has shaped me into who I am today. Without those struggles, I wouldn't have discovered my purpose or found the strength I carry now. And now, every single day, I get to watch the "seeds" I've planted take root in the lives of the teens I coach. When I see one of them step into their full potential, it feels like a victory—not just for them, but for me, too. This is what makes it all worth it— the chance to help others find their own strength and thrive. That's the true reward.

SCAN TO MEET AMANDA

# A PERSONAL THANK YOU
## FROM MEGAN DIRKS

This book wouldn't exist without the incredible humans who believed in it (and me) from the start. You've supported my creative chaos, the stressy setbacks, and the wild wins. You're all wildly different, and honestly, I know you'd drive each other nuts if I left you alone in a room for ten minutes... but I love you all fiercely. Your support, patience, and perfectly timed distractions kept me going. This project lives because of you.

\* \* \*

### HEATHER & ERIC
My parents that inspired me in very different ways, crafting the human I am today. I think I picked up the best of both of you. Thank you for always encouraging me to spread my wings and keep going.

### CHRIS
My husband that put up with my late-night ramblings, delays in our life goals, and a ridiculous amount of unpaid overtime that cut into our time together for over six months. You even became our podcast editor when I was spread too thin and imploding.

### MARY
For being the very first person I shared this idea with back in 2022, for seeing its potential, and for bravely becoming the first co-author to stand beside me with her story.

### MIKE
One of my favorite humans, plus the first person I felt safe sharing my before-and-afters with. You quieted my imposter syndrome, body image issues, and doubt so I could finally start for real in 2023.

# THE GOTL AUTHORS

I didn't expect to gain a bonus family from this. Some of you were close friends, some I barely knew, and most of you started as complete strangers. But somewhere along the way, you became my cheerleaders, collaborators, and co-dreamers. You trusted me with your stories and gave this project your raw, unfiltered vulnerability. *You* made this book powerful, I just organized it.

Many of you saw the vision: that this isn't just one book, but the beginning of something bigger. A movement. A stage for stories that have waited too long to be heard. From future volumes to live events, you helped breathe life into what GOTL could become and I'll never forget that.

# SHE RISES STUDIOS

A massive shoutout to the team at She Rises Studios. We fully expected to self-publish alone, not to find the most supportive and aligned team ever. Your editing team is phenomenal, Berna was my lifeline, and everyone who worked behind the scenes to bring this book to life. Hanna Olivas for giving my ladies opportunities to rise with magazine features, summit opportunities, and being welcomed into the entire SRS ecosystem. Your talent, dedication, and willingness to roll with my "one last tweak" moments mean the world.

# OUR EARLY SUPPORTERS

To our Kickstarter backers and pre-order supporters: *you* made this possible. This book exists because of your belief in it, and I couldn't be more grateful. You gave us little bursts of cash flow when we had none to polish this up even better.

You cheered, you pushed, you never let us quit.

Your names are forever a part of this journey:

## GOTL CHAMPIONS

*Anyone who supported us in extraordinary ways or above $100 in support.*

| | |
|---|---|
| *Lisa Callahan* | *Brenda Del Granado* |
| *Shonna Beckman* | *Marika Wessels* |
| *Diane Jacobs Natoli* | *Ron Natoli* |
| *Jodi Harty* | *Breanna Campbell* |
| *Nate Fraughton* | *Tania Rizoski* |
| *Cheryl Heller* | *Michelle Marie Lappin* |
| *Sharon Katz* | *Peggy Bouras* |

Michael Bouras
Lisa Blaszczyk
Joanna Shalleck-Klein
Mikaela Harty
Susan Donald
Ann Shalleck

Foti Gianniosis
Patricia Heller
Sarah MacIsaac
Sandra Del Granado
Jenny Rozelle
Joy Lowe

## EARLY SUPPORTERS

*Those who were with us from the very first time we called on you.*

Tracey MacCharles
Megan Potts
Lauren Smith
Devin Stein
Emily Medley
Jean-Luc Recoussine
Chip Thompson
Vasiliki Fitzmaurice
Sabine Kerael
Joanne Johnson
Amy Stone
Darlene Fraughton
Simone Muise
Janet Roebuck
Pam Dirks
Ellen Wilcox
Nicole Macauley
Michelle Chandler
Jo-Ann Glock
Nicole Macauley
Jane Kent
Benita Brucia
Brian Durand
Daniel Gundred
Scott Demarest
Kim Luret

Kate Price
Paul Tornetta
Travis Warren
Claire Patterson
Lacey Jablonski
Judy Thompson
Meredith Lockhart
Beatrice Recoussine
Hilary May
Kaleigh Rand
Jules de Bellefeuille Defoy
Paul Wilcox
Melissa Fraga
Gina Morgan
Debbie Mason
Olivia Strojcevski
Peter Rappa
Glenn Schineis
Janet Cullum
Dawn Green
Nina Liu
Nelson Torres
Karina Mosqueda
Fabi Perez
Patricia Bota
Whitney Fauth

Annemarie Dowd

Alexis Bouras

Barbara Harpuder

Marianne Bouras

Kevin Fitzmaurice

Anya Lisowski

Shannon Grochowski

Heidi Tacktill

Georgia Golfinopoulos

Christina Roberts

Megan LeBlanc

Kat Pohl

Fallon Fraser

Keri Natoli

Eric Emme

Jeremy Betancourt

Paula Wolf

Salvatore Puma

April Lark

Susan Donald

Marjorie Zink

Chrissy Sjoberg

Chrystina Lowe

Nick Holloway

Jacqueline Beaulac

Alfonso Estera

Stephanie P

Angela Adair

Beverly Ryan

Frank Natsis

Michelle Hutcheson-Tipton

Rachel Moebes

Lilia Murillo

Katie Noonan

Ana Pestana

Rebecca Kokoski

Marica Skurtevska

Jennie Von Ruden

Meredith Hodge

Cecilie Steinsland

Beth Hammett

Kassandra Tanguay

Gina Nicoletti

Thadeu Borges

Jean Schwartz

Lauren Troppmann

Jean Tesoriero

Floriane Wu

Karol Trikkis

Christine Zielinski

Angela Westgate

Amberly Polanco

Andrea Lenssen

Fransheska Del Granado

Danielle Gannon

Edmund Louie

And to *you*, the reader: whether you've been following my work for years or just stumbled into this world, thank you for being here. You're why stories matter. You're why *this* story matters.

# THE GIRL ON THE LEFT

The Girl On The Left was sparked by project creator Megan Dirks, who saw the need for women to face the past, messy, imperfect versions of themselves. As the host of *The Girl On The Left* podcast, Megan gives women a chance to step up, share their stories, and shine in their full, unapologetic glory.

GOTL is all about celebrating where you've been and giving credit to the girl who laid the foundation for who you are today. This movement puts women's stories from around the world on display, empowering all women everywhere to claim their narrative and own their journey.

# COME SEE WHAT WE DO

The Girl on the Left offers workshops, events, podcast features, and book opportunities to elevate women and share their stories. For more information, contact **hello@thegirlontheleft.com**

## SHARE YOUR STORY & EMPOWER WOMEN

We seek powerful stories from women whose voices deserve to be heard to be featured in the expansion of our podcast, books, and live events.

The Girl on the Left book is published in 13 countries, and our podcast is on all major podcasting platforms. Our authors offer board-certified coaching, speaking engagements, and workshops to inspire, elevate, and uplevel. Come share your #GOTL story today!